MW01628648

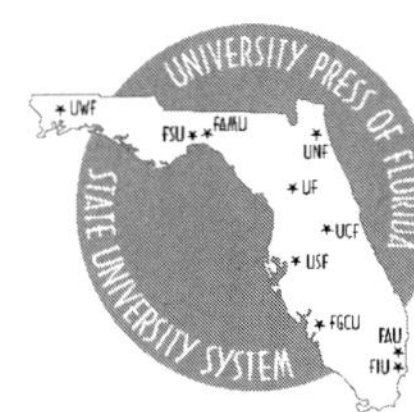

Florida A&M University, Tallahassee
Florida Atlantic University, Boca Raton
Florida Gulf Coast University, Ft. Myers
Florida International University, Miami
Florida State University, Tallahassee
University of Central Florida, Orlando
University of Florida, Gainesville
University of North Florida, Jacksonville
University of South Florida, Tampa
University of West Florida, Pensacola

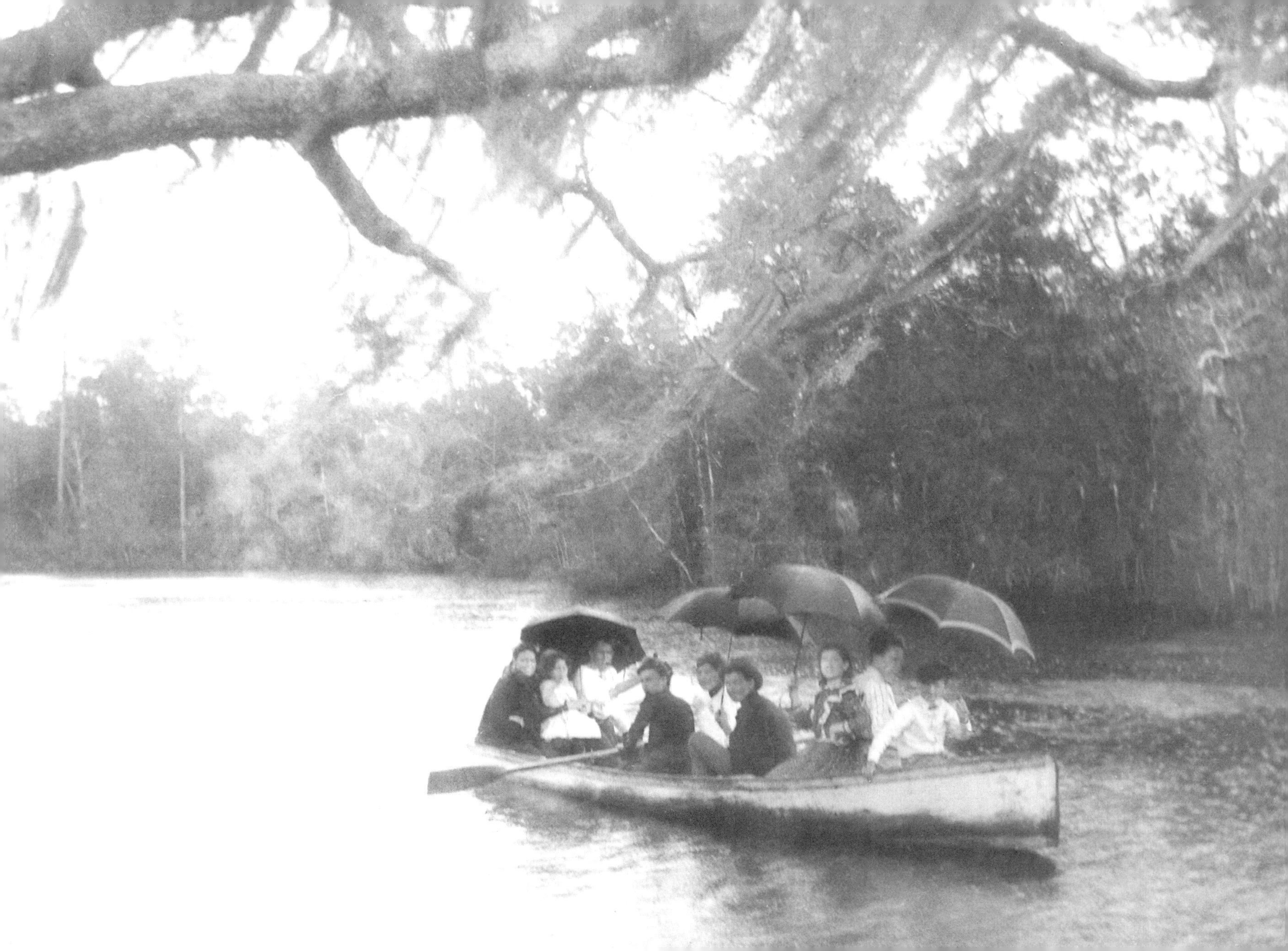

Jacksonville Greets the 20th Century

The Pictorial Legacy of Leah Mary Cox

Ann Hyman and photo editor, Ron Masucci

University Press of Florida

Gainesville · Tallahassee · Tampa · Boca Raton

Pensacola · Orlando · Miami · Jacksonville · Ft. Myers

Printed in the United States of America on acid-free paper

07 06 05 04 03 02 6 5 4 3 2 1

LIBRARY OF CONGRESS CATALOGING-IN-PUBLICATION DATA
Cox, Leah Mary, 1867-
Jacksonville greets the twentieth century: the pictorial legacy of Leah Mary Cox /
[compiled by] Ann Hyman and photo editor, Ron Masucci.
p. cm.
ISBN 0-8130-2548-6 (c.: alk. paper)
1. Jacksonville (Fla.)—History—20th century—Pictorial works. 2. Jacksonville (Fla.)—Social life and customs—20th century—Pictorial works. 3. Jacksonville (Fla.)—Buildings, structures, etc.—Pictorial works. I. Hyman, Ann. II. Masucci, Ron. III. Title.
F319.J1 C69 2002
975.9'12063'222—dc21   2002019471

The University Press of Florida is the scholarly publishing agency for the State University System of Florida, comprising Florida A&M University, Florida Atlantic University, Florida Gulf Coast University, Florida International University, Florida State University, University of Central Florida, University of Florida, University of North Florida, University of South Florida, and University of West Florida.

University Press of Florida
15 Northwest 15th Street
Gainesville, FL 32611-2079
http://www.upf.com

ILLUSTRATIONS

FOREWORD

Ann Hyman's accomplishment in bringing together the photographs of Leah Mary Cox adds to our knowledge and appreciation both of early-twentieth-century Jacksonville and of northeast Florida history. In this book, Hyman also tells the story of Cox herself, a remarkable woman born in England and brought up by her parents in Ohio, Nebraska, and Tallahassee, Florida. She moved alone to Jacksonville in 1888 as a young adult to earn her keep and learn the art of photography. Her pictorial legacy to the generations that followed shows this Florida city at the turn of the century in images that reflect the photographer's unique point of view of the places and people that set Jacksonville apart.

This collection is certain to enrich our understanding of the state's history. When Floridians themselves reflect upon the history of their state, they often tend to turn to elementary school memories or tourist-oriented images of sixteenth-century Spanish explorers searching for gold, expanding their empire, and perhaps longing for a fountain of youth. Once the peninsula came under the American flag, Florida—far from the federal government in Washington—simply became an appendage to the southern region that seceded from the Union in 1861. Florida in that year was largely frontier and had the smallest population of any of the Confederate states.

Modern Florida began with Henry Flagler's railroad, which ran down the east coast of Florida to Miami in the 1880s and 1890s and eventually reached Key West, and with Henry Plant's rail line across the state from Jacksonville to Tampa. Tourism during these years after the Civil War became an important part of the state's economy and character. After World War I, tourists and land speculators set off the Florida boom of the 1920s, as sightseers and new residents arrived by rail, ship, and model-T Ford. But even in 1940, on the eve of World War II, the state still had the smallest population in the region. The Sunshine State's surge to the position of fourth-largest state by population came only in the past sixty years. In many respects, present-day Florida, despite its early Spanish origins, ranks among the last-developed states of the Union.

One result of Florida's rapid recent growth is that Floridians have little sense of their history. The Spanish past seems unconnected to the present except in cities like St. Augustine. There are few recent historical remembrances whose stature compares with Philadelphia's Independence Hall, South Carolina's antebellum plantations, Virginia's Civil War battlefields, New York's Statue of Liberty, New Orleans's French Quarter, San Antonio's Alamo, or even San Francisco's Golden Gate Bridge.

It has been only in the past generation that scholars and others have begun seriously to create a sense of the state's history, examining the lives of cattlemen, cigar makers, Cubans, African Americans, Native Americans, women, governors, business tycoons, city builders, and others previously neglected. Historic preservation groups, particularly the Florida Trust and the Florida Humanities Council, have sponsored weekend excursions to encourage visits to towns and cities that began to flourish at the end of the nineteenth and beginning of the twentieth centuries. Local historical societies have done their part too. Floridians today are assembling their modern history piece by piece, and this book contributes to that effort.

Photographs of early-twentieth-century Florida are significant keys to understanding the state's relatively recent past. For Jacksonville, other than photos of the Great Fire of 1901 and commercial postcards that tourists mailed to friends and relatives back home in the freezing North, not many pictures remain that portray the city and its environs. This collection of photographs by Leah Mary Cox includes the fire, as well as the Ostrich Farm, Dixieland Amusement Park, Ft. George Island, beaches, St. Andrews Protestant Episcopal Church (now the restored home of the Jacksonville Historical Society), old St. Luke's Hospital (also restored), the Windsor Hotel and National Bank of Jacksonville, the police station, theaters, river vistas, and Gala Week.

They capture vignettes of daily life in the city before World War I, and they offer a sense of the vitality and diversity characteristic of Jacksonville, then the largest city in the state.

The 1901 Jacksonville fire became a turning point in local history—90 percent of downtown burned, and newcomers joined with long-term residents to rebuild a new, bigger, and better New South city when Miami was still little more than a village. Cox's photos capture the urban character of this city born again.

The photographs of the Ostrich Farm and Dixieland Amusement Park reflect the changing attitudes in Jacksonville and across the nation about work and play, as do her images of the new moving-picture theaters featuring stars like Mabel Paige, Mary Pickford, Lillian Gish, Oliver Hardy, and Charlie Chaplin. For a nickel, one could buy an evening's entertainment and fond memories. Part of the motion picture industry actually moved to Jacksonville for a decade before the war to shoot film for national distribution. Briefly the city became the "World's Winter Film Capital," until Hollywood took over year round.

Equally popular in season were trips to the seaside, first by train and later by car, to escape the summer heat. Sun seekers enjoyed auto racing on the hard-packed beaches and flocked to dance pavilions, restaurants, and overnight accommodations that ranged from campsites to the magnificent Continental Hotel. Some frequented Palmetto Lodge, the seaside annex to Cora Taylor Crane's famous brothel in town. And of course, there was the ocean. Cox's pictures capture glimpses of this new leisurely lifestyle enjoyed by visitors and by residents who could afford it.

Toward the end of November each year, thousands came to Jacksonville for a special holiday, Gala Week, with its parades of police and firefighters, militia, Shriners, marching bands, decorated floats, and automobiles. For Gala Week in 1900, there was a golf tournament at the country club, a circus performance opposite the railroad station, horse racing in Springfield, street shows, trapeze performers, and a Thanksgiving football game between the Jacksonville Light Infantry and a team from Macon, Georgia. Merchant Leopold Furchgott called the week "the biggest time ever in Jacksonville." Cox's photos capture much of the Gala Week spirit.

Cox also turned her photographer's eye on the natural environment of northeast Florida, one of the area's greatest attractions for residents and tourists alike. Its diversity also accounted for the movie industry's interest, with scenery that included rivers and creeks, the ocean, swamps, open fields, woodland, and bluffs. Passenger boats sailed up the St. Johns River to Green Cove, Palatka, and beyond on overnight and weekend excursions. Shrimping, crabbing, oystering, and casting for a variety of fish provided jobs and diversion for many.

What Cox's camera missed were Jacksonville's African Americans, a group comprising more than one-half of the population during this time. Their work and play, homes and churches, shops and schools also were part of the city. But Cox was a product of her era, when segregation tightened its bonds on southern society, and her omission of African Americans reflects less on her than on the region and times in which she lived.

Only in the past generation or so have historians and others begun to appreciate the role women played in the American past, as wives and mothers but also as pioneers, breadwinners, teachers, and community volunteers. Cox's life typified that of many young women of her day who moved from farm to city seeking a vocation (in Cox's case as a milliner) and becoming self-sufficient. For Cox, however, the challenges were even greater, and as Ann Hyman rightly points out, she was an extraordinary woman. The details of her life unfortunately are sketchy, but the overall picture is of a woman who not only survived, but also persevered, and who left a legacy for others to appreciate.

Cox, of course, was not the only extraordinary woman of her era. There were many in both the white and black communities. One group of relatively affluent women formed the Jacksonville Woman's Club. Under the leadership of Ada Cummer and her daughter-in-law Nina (benefactress of Jacksonville's Cummer Museum of Art and Gardens), May Jennings (wife of a former governor), Lina Barnett (wife of a bank president), Annie Broward (widow of a former governor), and others, the club pioneered private-sector initiatives in education (creating the first parent-teachers association), public health (combating tuberculosis), aid to the poor (hiring the first social workers), parks, prison reform, and community fund-raising, which later became the United Way.

Across the color line, Eartha Mary Magadelene White played a comparably extraordinary role as teacher, nurse, businesswoman, social worker, political activist, and founder of the Colored Old Folks Home, Clara White Mission, and first African American Red Cross chapter during the First World War.

In contrast to such community-oriented efforts, Cox led a more private life, perhaps typical of the artist/photographer. She had first to support a family; some of their descendants still live in the Fishweir Creek home. And she created this pictorial legacy of Jacksonville, which spans the years from 1900 to the First World War. The collection of her photographs uniquely captures the trauma of the fire, the spirit of Gala Week, the beauty of the environment, and the physical diversity of the city. In addition, the book includes two particularly welcome images of the photographer herself, as a young woman and mature adult. What a remarkable person she must have been!

Ann Hyman, journalist and author, has enhanced this collection of photographs with imaginative text, enriching the historical record of Jacksonville and northeast Florida.

James B. Crooks, University of North Florida

ACKNOWLEDGMENTS

This is a book of pictures. Making it was not so much a matter of finding words to tell the story of Leah Cox as it was a matter of seeing her story in her pictures. There is little written information about her life, and because most people who knew her are gone, or they knew her only slightly as an old, old woman who may have been a very different person from the young woman who took the pictures, writing about her becomes a matter of re-creating context.

Emily Lisska, executive director of the Jacksonville Historical Society and encourager of this project, focused immediately on the major intersections of Leah Cox's story with the Jacksonville story. Cox was in Jacksonville and, in fact, was personally affected by the city's "big three"—the terrible yellow fever epidemic in 1888, the Spanish-American War in 1898, and the Great Fire in 1901, the worst fire to hit a Southern city in the history of the country. Lisska's observation helped to establish the context of Cox's work.

Paul Karabinis, head of the photography department at the University of North Florida and keeper of the university's art gallery, was extremely helpful and generous with his time and insights. When I first heard the story of Leah Cox, I assumed that it was unusual for a woman to have been a photographer a hundred years ago. No. From the beginning, women took to photography, and Eastman Kodak recognized the market for the company's products among women. In fact, politically incorrect as they may sound today, early advertisements promised that photography was such a simple art, "even a woman" could master it. And, indeed women did, professionally and as hobbyists. Perhaps Leah Cox would have been among the professionals, if not for her circumstances, and her loyalty to family.

Florida Times-Union staff writer Bill Foley's work is an invaluable underpinning for anyone looking for the human—and often humorous—side of Jacksonville history. I owe him special thanks for finding actress Mabel Paige in order for her to have her brief curtain call in this book.

Dr. Wayne Wood, whose careful work has done so much to make the city's history known more broadly and deeply and to make it popular with a large audience of readers, has been supportive and encouraging.

It has been a special pleasure to meet and to work with members of Leah Cox's family in preparing this text. Nieces Lenah Geiger and Alice Jones and nephew Linus Scott have been helpful and generous in answering questions about events and people from so many years ago. Mary Jane Cox is due special thanks for having shared the few details that there are to share regarding Leah Cox's romance.

Mary Jane Cox's daughter, Susan Masucci, is also due special thanks, and, of course, Ron Masucci, the keeper of the photographs, is the person to whom special thanks from the community are due. Without his curiosity, his recognition of a treasure when he saw it, and his care in preserving and researching the thousands of glass negatives he discovered in Leah Cox's basement, we would not have her view of Jacksonville.

❧ 1 ❧

Modern photography stops action in midair. Click. But turn-of-the-century photography stopped time, absorbed an image, and transformed it into a still-life study, a portrait of an individual, a souvenir of an outing, or a record of a place. That is the essence of the work of Leah Mary Cox, whose photographs of Jacksonville at the end of the nineteenth century and in the opening decades of the twentieth century hold time captive.

Cox's work preserves images of amusement parks, streetcars, women in lace, men in jaunty straw hats, acolytes in white vestments, horses and buggies, Tin Lizzies heaped with flowers for a celebration, the city in ashes after it was almost destroyed by fire in 1901.

Alas, Leah Cox kept no journal or other written record of the circumstances of her photographs, so we don't know the process involved in choosing sites, or whether there were obstacles—physical or societal—for a woman setting up her camera to record the life of the city. We don't know whether she had a helper. But no written record of her experience is necessary to tell us that Cox had a precise and orderly mind.

That is visible in the way she kept track of her pictures, whether they record the aftermath of the Great Fire or serve as souvenirs of picnic outings or of a parade of soldiers on horseback, steamboats at the city docks or folks dressed in their Sunday best sailing on the St. Johns River.

Perhaps it's true of most photographers—certainly it's true of Leah Mary Cox—that you must look back through the photograph to the photographer, not the other way round. The photographer is, to borrow from St. Paul, seen through a glass darkly, and the glass is the lens of her camera. She is at the opposite end of the image. There must be material for an entire personality indicator in the answer to the question of whether an individual would rather be in the picture, or take the picture.

Evidence is overwhelming that Leah Cox would rather take the picture. She left a collection of more than four thousand glass negatives—but few images of herself.

Ron Masucci became fascinated by Leah Cox's photographs twenty years ago. Masucci is the husband of Susan Cox Masucci, a grandniece of the photographer. When Ron Masucci became restless at Sunday afternoon family gatherings, he retreated to the basement of the house Leah Cox built—where family members still live—and browsed through the boxes of glass negatives that she had, once upon a time, stored there.

Most were in good shape. They showed family and friends, along with scenes of Jacksonville, Tallahassee, St. Augustine, Miami, Fernandina, even Nebraska.

Masucci's initial interest in the glass negatives was their antiquity. He was not aware, at first, that photographs could be printed from the old glass negatives. He mentioned them to a photographer, and, when he learned they were usable, he began having prints made. That launched him into the history both of the region and of the Cox family. He learned about the city and the Cox family, but Leah Cox remained in the background, behind her lens.

"Nobody knows anything about her," Masucci reflected. "One person will tell you she was mean or tough, but, the things she did, she had to be that way. She recorded a lot of history and her intention was for it to live on."

The history is there, the context of the times, in Leah Cox's work. Inevitably, the photographs record Cox's life and the life of her family. But the photographer is not in them often. Cox always stood behind the camera. Was she elusive? Shy? A fugitive soul? Not necessarily. Behind the camera is where she had to be to get the picture. It may be as simple as that.

2

A photographer's vision begins to be shaped long before she picks up her first camera. There must be an innate tendency to frame experience, to edit what is to be kept in memory. It must happen long before there is the vocabulary to describe the process.

Leah Cox was eight years old when her family—parents William Henry Cox and Ellen Jaggersmyth Cox, sister Esther, and brother William—left Newberg, Ohio, and headed west, part of a sea of pioneers who flooded out of the east as if some giant hand had tipped the continent toward the Rockies. Thousands set out, looking for new beginnings in the western lands being opened up for settlement. Kansas, Oklahoma, Nebraska, and the Dakotas were there for the taking. The government lured folks west with the lofty notion of Manifest Destiny and cheap, even free, and sometimes worthless land, the product of the so-called log cabin legislation that, with modifications, lasted from the Homestead Act of 1862 until 1977. The hopeful settlers did not fear hardship or know how tough making it in the West would be and how many of the newcomers would eventually come back east again.

The Cox family, restless for the opportunity promised in the West, had been in America only a few years when they moved from Ohio to Nebraska. They had come to America in 1872, sailing from Liverpool, England, to New York in May aboard the *Great Western*, a steam packet, one of the first steam-powered ships to cross the Atlantic.

Leah—born June 15, 1867—was almost five when the family set off on its great migration across the ocean. There is no way to see the voyage, likely two weeks at sea, through the eyes of a bright, curious five-year-old. She was a child with a special vision that would eventually be so evident in her photography. The little girl must have absorbed that experience of ocean, of journey, of the unknown quite fully and stored it somewhere in her head as a resource, a reference. When she got to the Great Plains of Nebraska (Valparaiso and Fremont), it's not difficult to imagine Leah Cox seeing the land as she had seen the ocean on her voyage, the earth a still, negative image of the perpetual motion of the sea.

Lenah Geiger, a niece of Leah Cox, recalled the Coxes' Nebraska years in a brief memoir she wrote in 1998: "The family lived in a sod house at first. They experienced a cyclone which lifted the house and carried it away, dust storms, prairie fires. The family grew in Nebraska, and Leah went to school in Nebraska for about five years."

Between blizzards and planting and harvests and distances between homesteads and town, pioneer children did not attend school as regularly as the seasons. They couldn't be sent off far from home in winter for fear of storms that seemed to come out of nowhere and could strand—and for that matter, freeze—travelers caught away from home. Prairie schools, in the country and in towns, were in session when it was possible—a term here, a term there, when space and a teacher could be found. Between terms, children studied their readers and practiced their numbers and letters. Readin', writin', and 'rithmetic were irregularly doled out and highly prized.

After ten years, the Cox family left Nebraska. "In 1885, when she [Leah] was 18, eldest of six children, the family, thinking the weather would be better for the Mother (sickly with a goiter) left Nebraska for Tallahassee, Florida," Lenah wrote.

Often, women did not fare well as pioneers. Many had traded comfortable cottages in Ohio or Iowa or West Virginia or Kentucky for sod dugouts and claim shanties on the Plains. Writers of the time regularly noted the killingly hard work, the uncertainty, the isolation even when dealing with sickness and childbirth that made women old before they were forty.

The Cox family would not be alone when it moved back east to look for an easier living for the brood. They chose Tallahassee because Henry Cox's brother, George

Cox, and his wife, Jane, who was Ellen's sister, were living there. The families lived on neighboring farms near Mud Lake and Silver Lake, a few miles southwest of Tallahassee.

Years later, Leah Cox passed on her memories of those years: Mud Lake had alligators, and Silver Lake was pretty. She remembered pitching in with the farmwork, riding bareback, and herding stock.

The vegetables they grew in Florida's sandy soil tasted poor after the vegetables she had pulled from Nebraska's rich dirt, she said. And, the water was bad. They boiled it before they drank it, and they made tea with it rather than drink it plain. (Perhaps it was sulfur water, definitely an acquired taste.) Ah, but the citrus. In England, in Ohio, in Nebraska, an orange in a child's Christmas stocking was a sign of the season. Special. Dear. In Florida, the trees were hung with golden fruit as if decorated for Christmas. On spring nights, the fragrance from the orange blossoms drifted across the lot, onto the front porch, and through the open windows, and it was the sweet breath of heaven, unlike anything Leah Cox had ever experienced.

Still, she was sometimes homesick for the Plains. After all, she had put down roots and grown up with the Nebraska landscape in her head, with Nebraska's good pioneer folk as neighbors, teachers, playmates. But she also remembered—who could forget?—the wind and the cold that Laura Ingalls Wilder, the classic chronicler of nineteenth-century pioneer life, would one day describe as cold "as terrible as silence."

There was no cold like that to dread in Florida, and the Cox family settled by the lakes, transplanted for the third time in Leah Cox's life.

Tallahassee was a lively, sociable little city where fortunes were sought and deals were made. Then, as now, Florida was a promised land of sorts, always on the make, paradise for sale. For decades after the Civil War, the state was a magnet for winter visitors and for new settlers. In the 1880s, Florida was hungry for the wealth, the progress, the possibility of prosperity that came with growth and development. Florida wanted railroads—and the railroads wanted Florida.

In that mutual hunger, Florida was no different from the western frontier that pushed across the Great Plains. There were no other apparent parallels. Nebraska was arctic. Florida was subtropical.

Nebraska was new to European settlement. The Plains were broken for the first time by the pioneers. Indian culture, and resistance to white settlement and transformation of the land, had not faded from the Plains—the Battle of the Little Bighorn, usually seen as the last major battle between Indians and the United States, was fought in 1876. In the East, however, including Florida, hostile Indians were a fading memory, history. It had been fifty years since the Seminole were forced into the Everglades or rounded up and sent west. Florida was pacified.

Though the state was sparsely settled, and distances between settlements were great, Florida's European history was the oldest in North America. The state's oldest city, St. Augustine, was a half-century older than Jamestown or Plymouth. The Florida story was a four-hundred-year tug-of-war among the Spanish, Indians, French, English, and American settlers, each with a flag to plant, a culture to champion.

When the Cox family arrived in Florida in 1885, the state's population was about 300,000, divided more or less equally between blacks and whites. Leon County, where Tallahassee lies, was the state's most populous county, with about 20,000. Major urban areas were Jacksonville, Key West, and Tampa—all port cities.

The state's great assets were its climate and the vast tracts of public land it could give away. Its main business was agriculture; others high on the list were development, and hospitality as a winter resort and a health retreat. Many northerners, after the Civil War, could afford travel and investment. Then, as ever since the industrial revolution, the middle class was on the rise, and the nation was restless. Florida looked like the main chance to thousands. A social observer noted that the rich came to Florida by luxury steamships that ran regularly along the Atlantic coast between New York and

Jacksonville, while the middle class traveled, less luxuriously, by rail. The poor came, too, often by wagon, driving stock and trailing dogs, looking for cheap land to clear and farm or plant with a grove, looking for new beginnings.

The main thing the state needed to accommodate major growth was transportation, specifically railroads. Roads were poor to nonexistent, distances great. Only the rivers and their tributaries offered dependable networks for moving through the country. Tons of manufactured and agricultural goods moved on the St. Johns River, a huge system that accounted for more than a thousand miles of navigable water. Other important systems included the Indian River, and the Ocklawaha, Apalachicola, Ochlockonee, Perdido, Suwannee, St. Marys, Withlacoochee, Peace, Caloosahatchee, Kissimmee, and Manatee.

The state needed money, too—investors and lenders. Businesspeople and farmers could not afford to follow Polonius's good advice to his son—"neither a borrower nor a lender be."

A sturdy branch of the publishing industry of the times produced an ever expanding list of Florida books—guides for tourists, would-be settlers, farmers curious about the citrus business and winter vegetables, invalids, merchants, carpenters, bankers, fishers, hunters. Just about everyone who could take pen in hand wanted in on the phenomenon, from unknown pamphleteers and hacks to famous writers. Harriet Beecher

Stowe, probably America's most famous writer of the day, wrote *Palmetto Leaves* in 1873, a come-on-down collection of sketches of life at her orange grove in Mandarin and of picnics, excursions, and characters in the environs of Jacksonville, St. Augustine, and along the St. Johns River. The great poet of the marshes of Glynn, Sidney Lanier, wrote a guidebook to Florida at the behest of the Atlantic Coast Line Railroad.

George Barbour, a writer for the *Chicago Times*, was part of the press corps that accompanied former president U. S. Grant on his 1879 tour of Florida. Barbour was hooked on Florida, and his 1882 book *Florida for Tourists, Invalids, and Settlers* has its peculiarities—he's very hard on the "crackers" and almost as intolerant of African American laborers. But leave aside the sociology of the day, and the book is widely considered to be the straight talk about Florida and a settler's prospects for prosperity. The subtitle alone hints at the breadth of Barbour's research. He promises—and generally delivers—key information on "climate, soil, and productions; cities, towns, and people; the culture of the Orange and other tropical fruits; farming and gardening, scenery and resorts; sport; routes of travel, etc. etc." "Etc. etc.," indeed.

Florida, like the rest of the Civil War–disrupted South, was still suffering socially, politically, and economically twenty years after the end of the conflict, but it was also a land of promise. The Cox family moved into a poor state, but a state that, like Nebraska, welcomed newcomers as harbingers of eventual prosperity.

Clearly, the books, taken along with other factors favoring growth and expansion after the Civil War, worked. The growth of the state was stunning between the end of the war and the beginning of the twentieth century. It was downright staggering beginning with the 1881–1885 administration of Governor William Bloxham.

The Cox family was part of the movement, following the sun—and of course, Aunt Jane and Uncle George Cox—to Florida.

Tallahassee was the city set on a hill, literally and figuratively. The state capitol dominated the little city from its site on the town's highest hill. It brooded, as a hen over its chicks, above an old, gracious, almost bucolic scene.

"It is an unpretentious old city, with an air of village-like rustic simplicity; no factories (except one cotton mill); all is quiet, country life," Barbour wrote.

> *The residence avenues are mostly lined with cozy little cottages, and comfortable, roomy, but substantial mansions of the good old-time style of architecture, and all are surrounded by neatly fenced lawns and gardens, almost all having quite ample grounds, well kept—and flowers, flowers, flowers! . . . The suburbs are everywhere lovely, and the views from the streets or house-tops—especially the roof of the State House—are exceedingly fine. The surrounding country is a vast range of hills, valleys, brooks, lakes, park-like clusters of large trees, broad, well-cultivated fields, large plantation dwellings and cotton-gins, and*

distant forest—in all, a remarkably beautiful natural panorama of nature, such as is seen nowhere else in Florida.

Barbour was taken with Tallahasseans, too.

"Nowhere, it may be said, is there a more refined and cultured society than in Tallahassee. Among them are many descendants of the most prominent and aristocratic old families of America, with names that recall old colonial, revolutionary, and 1812 days in the battlefields and in State councils; and their large, well-attended schools, numerous, handsome churches, beautiful homes and surroundings, attest to the high standard of the best society of Tallahassee."

There were alligators bellowing in the dark outside Leah's window, but the Cox family had moved from a frontier to an old, comfortable society when they moved to Florida.

Leah Cox was grown, eighteen, when her family came to Tallahassee. Her mother, Ellen Cox, was ailing. Leah, the eldest of the six children, was handed, and accepted, it turned out, a lifetime of heavy responsibility for her family. She tended stock and the garden. She supervised—and not simply supervised but prepared—meals for the family. She made sure the younger ones were up and out the door for chores or school.

Her father, William Henry Cox, mixed farming with carpentry to earn the family's living.

But life in Tallahassee was not without its social side.

Leah Cox made friends, perhaps through church. It is likely that her lifelong habit of church attendance was firmly in place by the time the family came to Florida. She would be a staunch Episcopalian always, and Tallahassee's venerable St. John's parish was a magnet, then as now, for the city's faithful and for those looking for fellowship and connection. There is every reason to believe that Leah Cox and the Cox family sought out the friendships and social opportunities provided by the parish.

We know that Leah Cox made friends in Tallahassee, because years later she would tell her niece that she left Tallahassee to come to Jacksonville to join friends who were already in Jacksonville.

There must have been conflicting impulses behind that decision to move.

The conflict was not complicated. The choice was between remaining in place in the family where she played a central role, or moving on with her life into independence. Freedom versus the ties that bind.

It's an American dilemma, fed by a national character that sees moving on as something of a personal manifest destiny, a search for the place in the sun, which implies, of course, getting out of the shadow cast by family expectations.

Leah Cox wanted her place in the sun. And she was shaped by a family that, like much of the rest of the country, did not shrink from moving on. They didn't traipse aimlessly from England to Ohio to Nebraska to Florida, but they did not put down roots so deep and entangling that they could not pull up and move on. The time came for Leah Cox to move on.

Friends urged her to come to Jacksonville—two hundred miles away—to learn a trade, dressmaking and millinery. She wanted it, wanted a new place, wanted work besides tending stock, house, and folks. She was hungry for a taste of independence. But there was an ailing mother and all those mouths to feed and buttons to mend at home. Could she really go? She made the decision. Yes, she would go, and she would return if her family sent for her.

Did her family support her in her decision to break away? We can suppose that it was a tough choice for Leah Cox, and it must have been tough for her parents and her younger siblings. We know that, to this day, the Cox family sticks together. They keep up with one another.

But, whatever the process and difficulty of decision for Cox, whether her family supported or opposed the move, she made the decision and she made the move. Leah Cox bought her ticket to Jacksonville, probably on the Savannah, Florida and Western Railroad, and the Jacksonville, Pensacola and Mobile line, a long day's journey.

3

In 1888, Jacksonville was Florida's premier city, socially and commercially. Its population was more than 15,000 and growing rapidly. It was a major winter resort.

Chicago Times reporter George Barbour's description tended toward the highly enthusiastic:

> *It is a handsome and prosperous-looking city, covering a good deal of ground, and, particularly during the winter season, when all the hotels are thrown open to the thronging guests, it presents an animated and picturesque appearance that is quite exceptional at the South.*
>
> *The streets are remarkably wide, and are nearly all shaded by long rows of mammoth live-oaks, forming spreading arcades of embowering green in winter as well as in summer. Good sidewalks of brick or planks contribute greatly to the comfort of pedestrians, but the streets themselves are too sandy for rapid or pleasant driving. . . .*
>
> *Bay Street is the principal business thoroughfare, and runs parallel to and one block distance from the river. For a distance of about a mile it is lined on both sides with stores, offices, and other mercantile buildings, including several of the leading hotels. The Astor*

Building at the corner of Bay and Hogan streets is the finest in the city, and in it, besides several stores and a number of offices, is the United States Signal Service station.

Horse cars connected the railroad depots with downtown hotels. There were at least two public markets, and even a souvenir shop and a free menagerie for the entertainment and edification of citizens and winter visitors.

The city was lit with gaslights. There was a water system drawing water from a field of artesian wells, and there was a sanitary sewer system. There were schools of good reputation and Episcopal, Presbyterian, Methodist, Baptist, and Catholic churches. There were musical and entertainment events. The steamboats from the North brought snowbird musicians to winter gigs, and the musicians brought the newest songs from New York City to play at hotel musicales and ballrooms. This population of professional musicians added a measure of sophistication to the city, and, as a bonus, it meant that the churches and other civic organizations had unusually fine music. There were newspapers, banks, a library, and shipping interests—most of Florida's rail and steamer lines were headquartered at Jacksonville, and great quantities of fruit, vegetables, lumber, cotton, and sugar moved through the city and its port.

New Yorker Wanton S. Webb, a well-known compiler of facts about cities to aid travelers, businesspeople, and investors, was high on the city Leah Cox chose:

The city of Jacksonville stands upon the great St. Johns River of Florida, at a point where . . . the Ocean, the River and the Railways meet.

It is the commercial capital of Florida.

It is the largest winter resort of the United States.

It is the centre of the wholesale trade of Florida.

It is a centre for fruit-packing and shipping.

It has lumber, cigar and other manufactures.

It is the railway centre of the State.

It is the termini of seven railways.

Its hotels are the finest and most comfortable in the South.

It has twenty hotels that during the past season (1886–87) registered more than 65,000 persons. . . .

Its increase in population during the past year has been more per percent than any city of equal or larger size in the world. . . .

It is by rail, only thirty-six hours from New York City, twenty hours from New Orleans, thirty-six hours from Cincinnati, and forty-nine hours from Chicago.

It is a city of churches. . . .

It is lighted both by gas and electricity, has a fire alarm telegraph and an efficient paid fire department.

It has telegraph and telephones.

Granting that such civic promotion was the convention of the day, Webb's description of Jacksonville was impressive and bound to catch the interest of people considering relocation, investment, or a winter vacation.

The Subtropical Exposition, which opened in January 1888, drew great numbers to the city—including President Grover Cleveland and Mrs. Cleveland. The presidential visit, on February 22, Washington's birthday, was dubbed Jubilee Day, and the president was the centerpiece of a parade that moved from the St. James Hotel to the exposition. The president and the first lady rode in a carriage filled with flowers and pulled by a team of six powerful jet-black horses wearing red, white, and blue streamers on their bridles.

At the exposition grounds, constructed especially for the fair at Waterworks Park at Main and First Streets, the presidential party was met by a crowd of common folks and by dignitaries led by Col. J. J. Daniel, one of the city's most distinguished citizens, the organizers of the exposition, and the publisher of the *Florida Times-Union* newspaper.

That evening, at a reception for the president and Mrs. Cleveland at the St. James Hotel, the crowd was so large that a staircase almost collapsed.

The exposition and the continuous receptions, dances, concerts, excursions, and entertainments for tourists were not important to Leah Cox simply because of their glamour. Dressmakers and milliners prospered in the city, and apprentices came eagerly to Jacksonville to learn the couture trades from accomplished dressmakers. There were, almost daily, advertisements in the newspaper classifieds seeking dressmakers and tailors. Experts offered instruction to apprentices. It was a lively trade.

But it seems an unlikely trade for a young woman who had ridden bareback to gather her family's livestock, a woman who would, in future years, climb rickety roofs and charred trees to get her photographs of a city ruined by fire. But dressmaking is what she chose.

Leah Cox was twenty-one when she stepped off the train from Tallahassee, and Jacksonville must have been daunting after the sleepy little capital city.

She hesitated a moment, spotted her friends across the depot platform, waved, and plunged into independence. It was a heady moment as she stepped over the threshold of a new life, a moment of myriad possibilities.

4

Leah moved in with friends on the east side, intent on learning the skills of a professional seamstress. She meant to prosper, to live an independent life. Immediately, she began to discover her way around the city—the hotels, the docks, the train stations, the city markets, the shops. She took an excursion on the *Queen of the St. Johns*, saw the Jacksonville White Stockings play baseball at the fairgrounds. She went to the Park Opera House. She rode the mule-drawn trolley from downtown to the Subtropical Exposition when bands, magicians, and theater troupes played special engagements. Fifty cents a show, twenty-five for a matinee—not an easy sum to come by, but a sum well spent.

An hour or two in Everett Park, across from the Everett Hotel, was free. There was a bandstand, orange and lemon trees, roses. Eagles, deer, monkey-faced owls—said to have been hatched in the dungeon at the old Spanish fort in St. Augustine—were on exhibit. Curios and flowers were for sale at a shop in the center of the park. Leah went to her dressmaking and millinery lessons in the drafty upstairs workroom of a shop within a ten-minute walk of the grand St. James Hotel.

In her early days in Jacksonville, as Leah Cox tried on a life of independence, she also experimented with the fashions of the era—hats of her own design, long gloves, a feather fan, a parasol, a cameo.

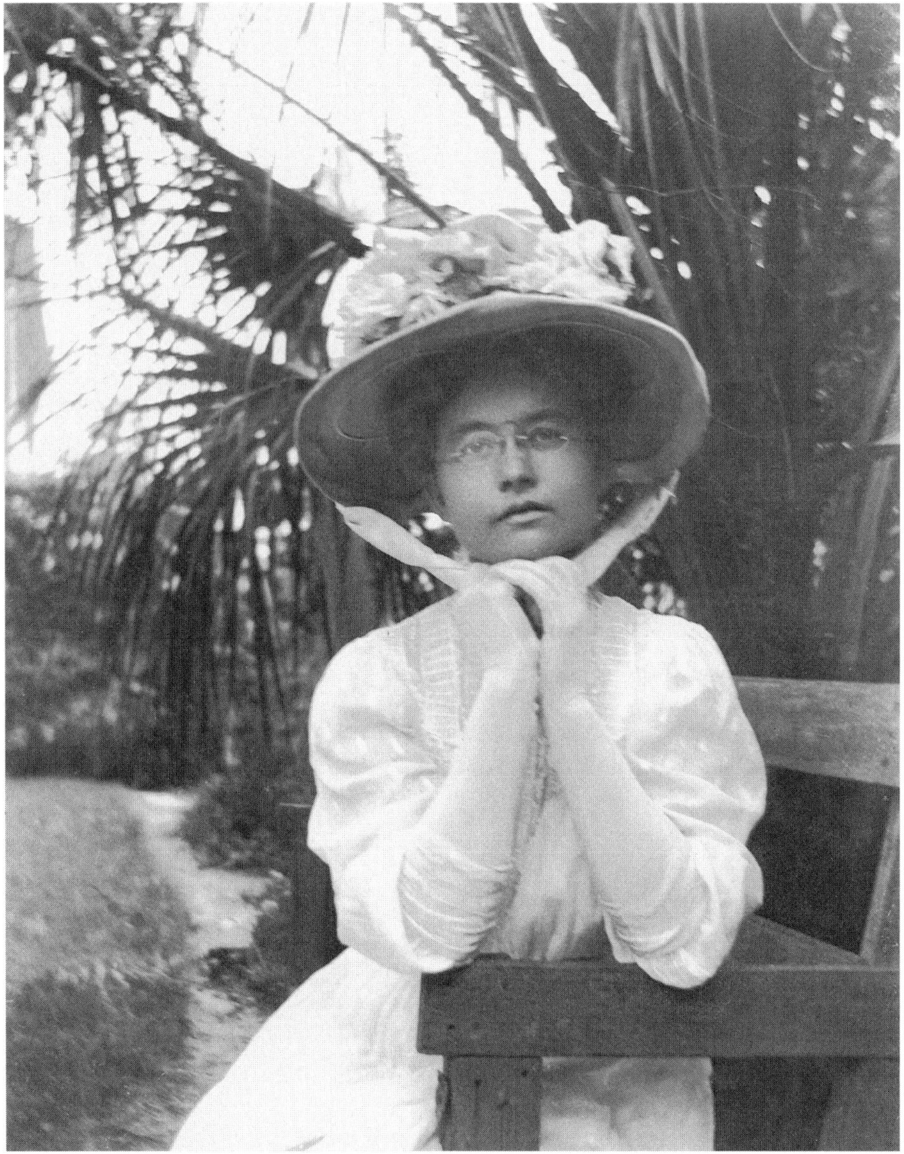

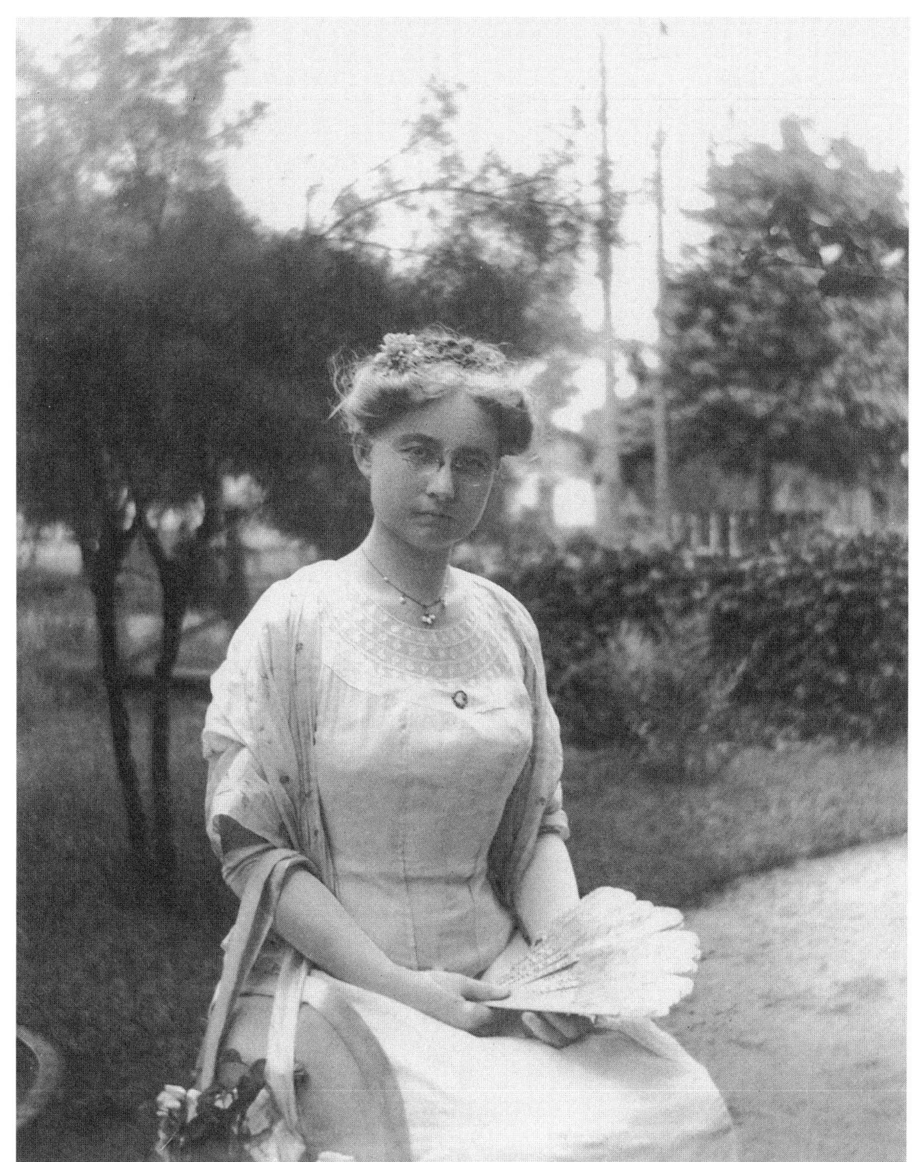

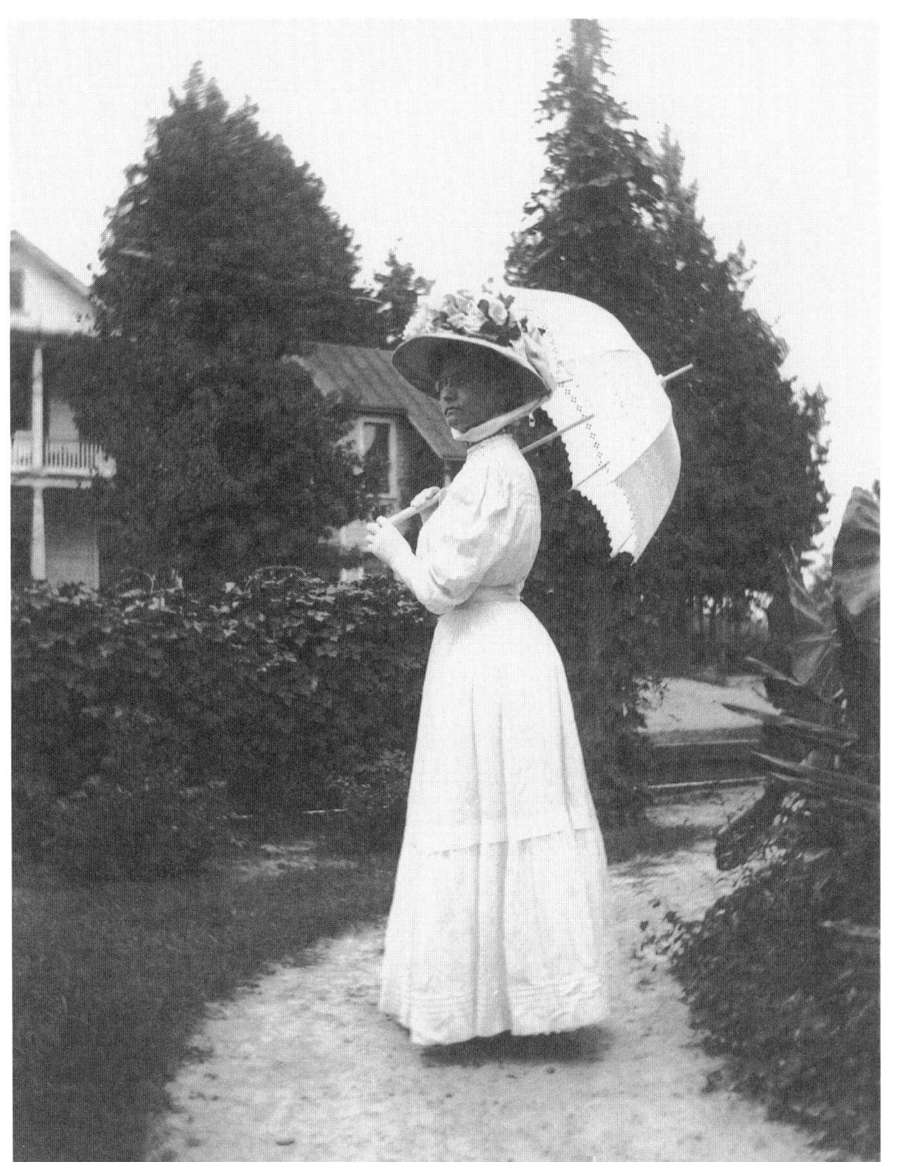

Facing page
Riverboats carried freight, passengers, and tourists on the St. Johns River. Jacksonville was a port city, one of the most important on the East Coast.

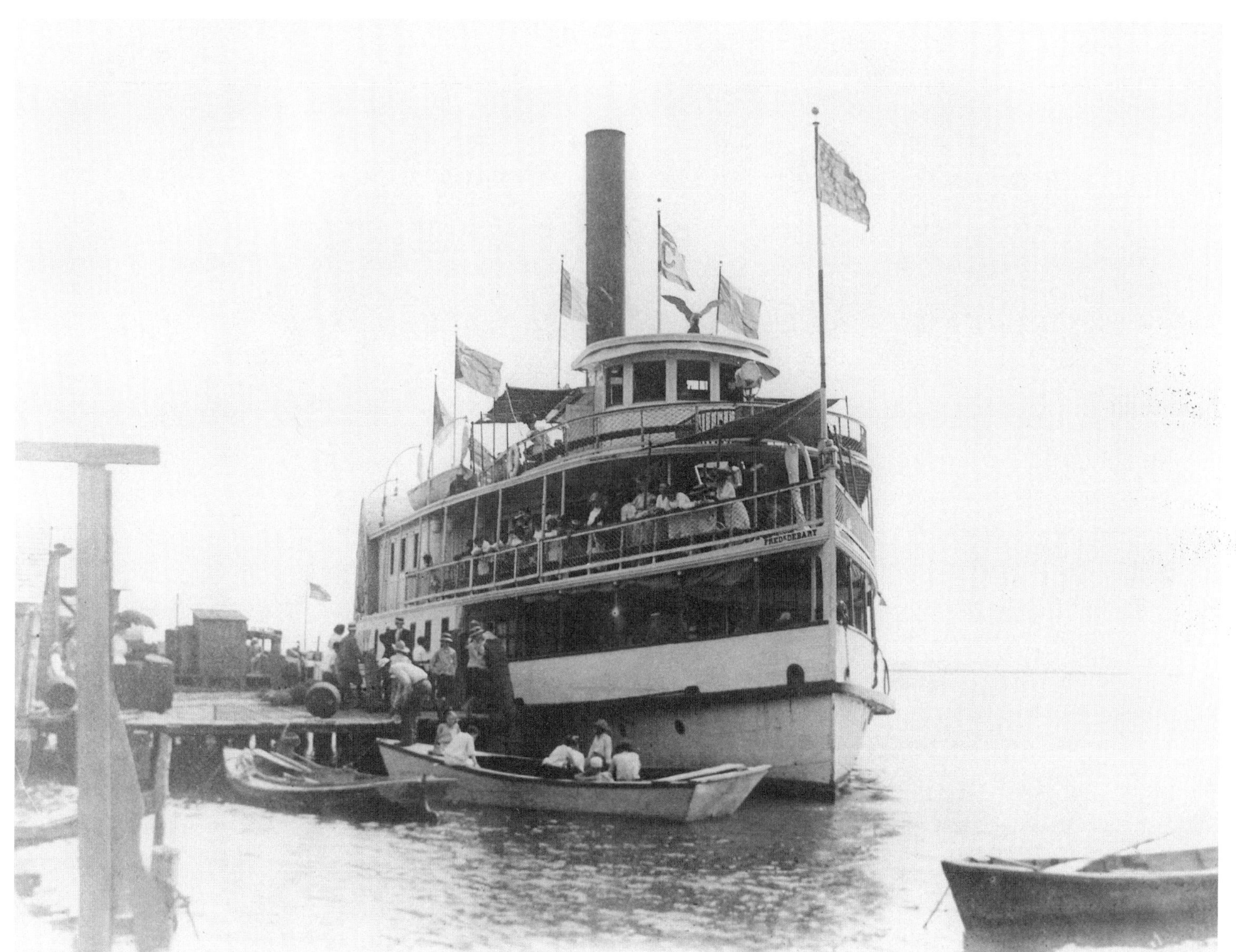
FRED^K DEBARY

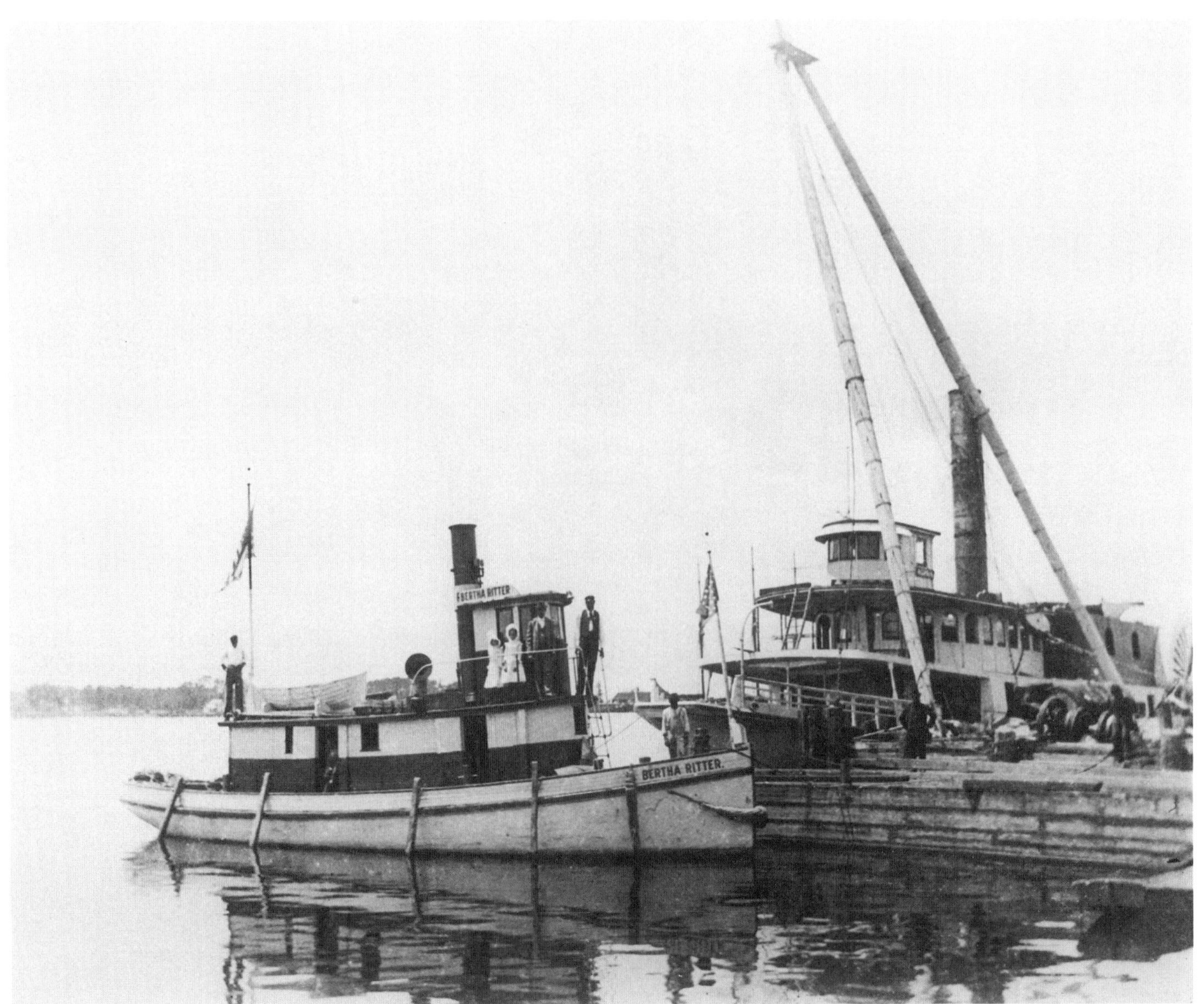
BERTHA RITTER
BERTHA RITTER.

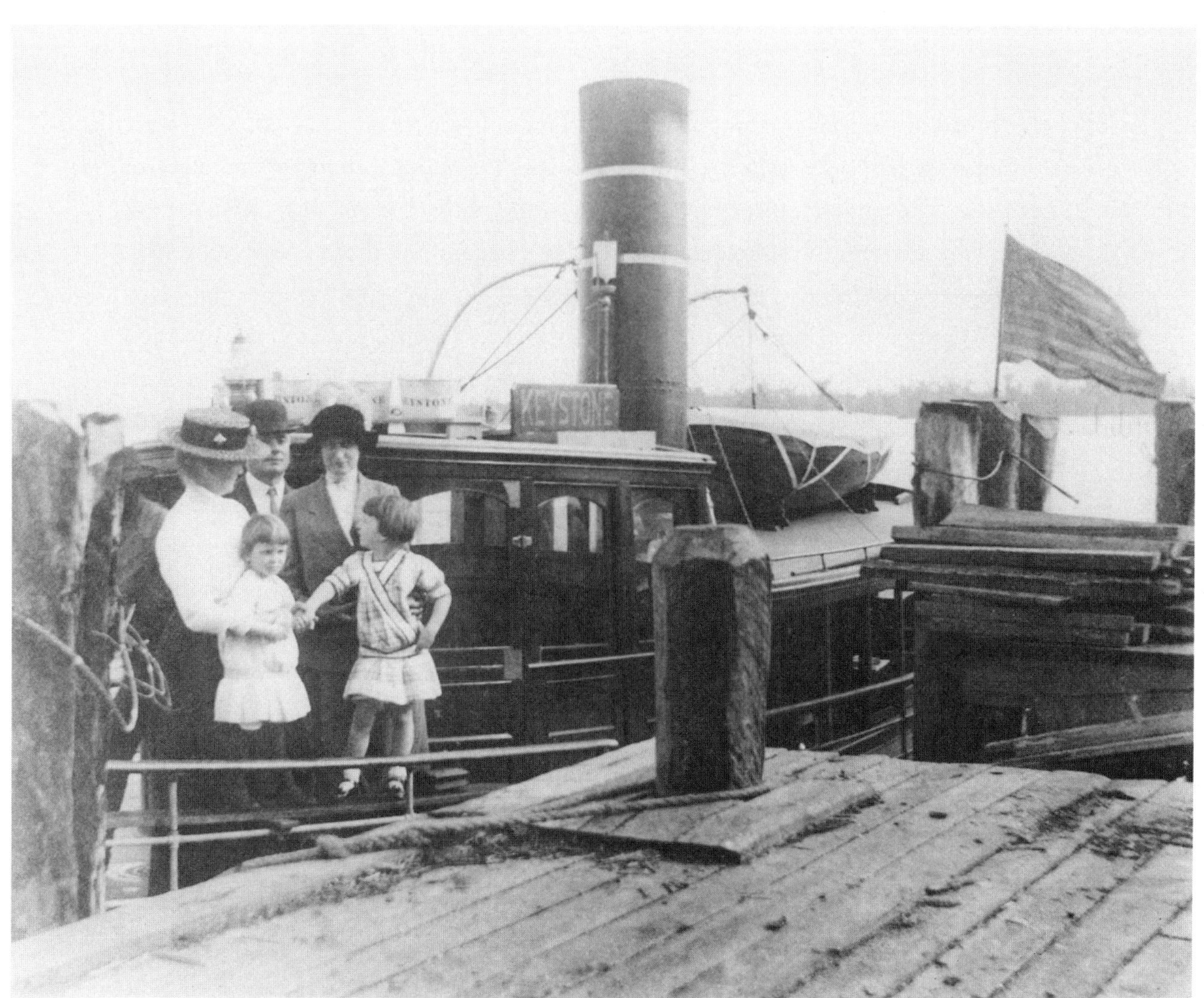

The changing scene of riverboats and small steamers on the river and at the docks drew Leah Cox and her camera to the riverfront again and again.

Leah had never seen anything like the St. James. It was world famous, and it was a world unto itself. There were five hundred rooms for guests. There was an elevator. There was a telegraph office, ticket agency, wine shop, barber shop, and reading rooms. The restaurant was famous—and elegant, beyond the means of an apprentice seamstress and her friends. They could only press their noses to the glass.

The Windsor, the Everett, and the Carleton House were also famous. And there were others, more than twenty hotels in all to serve thousands of tourists who were attracted by climate and reputation and well-known accommodations to the "Winter City in Summerland."

Everyone in Jacksonville was a people-watcher, the locals intrigued with the exotic visitors, who occasionally included even royalty, and the visitors intrigued with the locals. Visiting writers seldom failed to include descriptions and reflections on the natives, black and white. Wanton Webb did so, not kindly. Harriet Beecher Stowe saw the locals with gentler eyes, except for the "parcel of hulking fellows" on a steamer excursion on the St. Johns River—"the sweetest paradise God ever made." The offenders kept up a "constant fusillade upon every living thing that shows itself on the bank. Now a bird is hit, and hangs, head downward, with a broken wing; and a coarse laugh choruses the deed. Now an alligator is struck; and the applause is greater." H. L. Mencken wrote about the people of Jacksonville when he was sent to the city by his

Baltimore newspaper in the aftermath of the 1901 fire. In latter days, Marjorie Kinnan Rawlings's description of her rural Florida neighbors was the soul of her work.

In her time, Leah Cox would document Jacksonville and its people too, through her photographs, but in the beginning, she could only watch and explore her new territory.

Cox joined St. Andrew's Episcopal Church, something of a newcomer to the city too, inasmuch as the first services held by the parish were on Easter 1888. Cox happily became involved in the work of the new church. She attended worship services and social events, and even built kneelers for the choir stalls in the sanctuary. In her lifetime, she took hundreds of photographs of the church—and she also toted covered dishes to parish suppers and brought buckets of flowers for the altar.

In her first months in Jacksonville, Cox shared space, a furnished room, with friends who had also made the move from Tallahassee to Jacksonville to seek their fortune. But the search for independence and a new life, at least with unfettered optimism, did not last for her.

A grim setback that no one had counted on, and no one could hold off, was gathering like doomsday on Jacksonville's horizon. And within the larger tragedy, the Cox family would suffer a loss that would change Leah Cox's future. Independence would suddenly disappear as an option for the young woman.

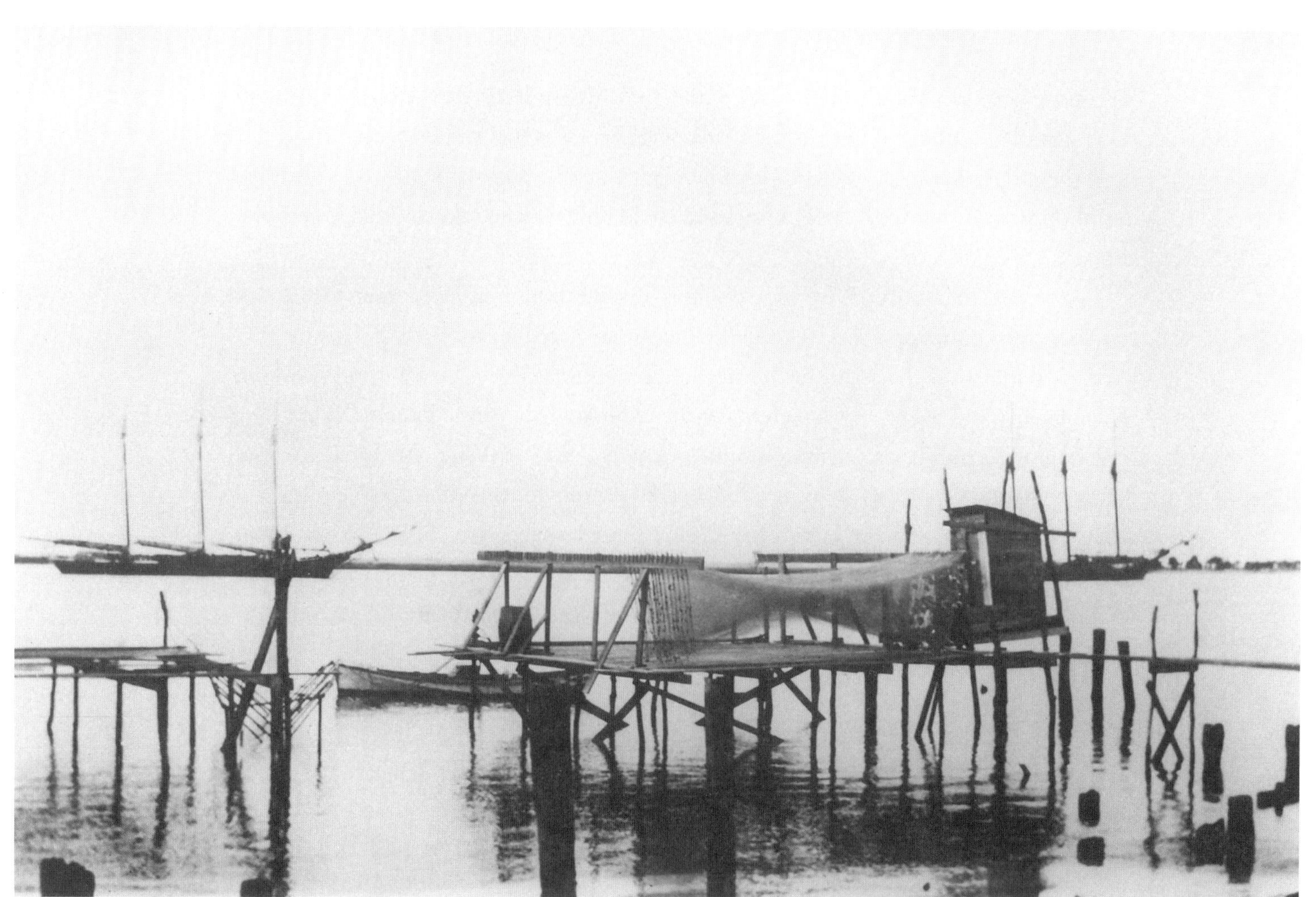

Commercial mullet and shrimp fishing nets, draped to dry along the river's edge.

Yellow fever was the thief. Within months of Cox's arrival, Jacksonville would become a plague city and its people would become pariahs, turned away from virtually every city in the Southeast, as far away as Tennessee and Kentucky. Shotgun posses went so far as to threaten to tear up railroad tracks from Jacksonville if a train approached their town bringing refugees or goods, even mail, from the stricken city.

Yellow fever was not uncommon in the South, hitting some cities, especially New Orleans, again and again. When it occurred, it was devastating, not only to the health of a city, but also to civic life. Transportation and thus trade ended when yellow fever struck. People feared it as their thirteenth-century ancestors feared the plague. And for good reason. Though its mortality rate was unpredictable—mild cases came and went disguised as flu—yellow fever's toll could be horrendous. In *Yellow Fever and the South*, author Margaret Humphreys provides a clinical description of the disease:

> *Classic yellow fever begins with the abrupt onset of shaking chills, fever, and muscle aches. This is followed by liver failure and jaundice, giving the fever its name. Hepatic congestion combined with systemic dysfunction of the clotting system causes hemorrhage from the gums, nose, and stomach lining. When vomited this digested blood looks black; the Spanish name for yellow fever is vomito negro. Renal failure as evidenced by the cessation of urine output, precedes death by one to two days. In fatal cases, death occurs in about a week. Estimates of mortality range from ten to sixty percent of those infected.*

Yellow fever was sometimes called the "Stranger's Disease" because people who grew up in the yellow fever–prone cities of the South (yellow fever is an urban, not a rural, disease) had often acquired immunity from having had the disease as children. Youngsters who contract the disease generally do not get as sick with it as adults do, and thus they are quite likely to escape death, and future infection.

A stranger brought yellow fever to Jacksonville in 1888. It came to town with a saloon keeper from Tampa, R. D. McCormick, who, with his wife and daughter, checked into the Grand Union Hotel for a brief stay to visit relatives in Jacksonville.

McCormick did not feel well when he checked into the hotel on July 28, 1888, and he asked to see a doctor. The doctor diagnosed the traveler's illness as "intermittent fever." However, when McCormick did not improve but seemed, in fact, to grow worse, the hotel keeper sent word to Neal Mitchell, head of the Duval County Board of Health. As it happened, Joseph Y. Porter, a physician from Key West who was considered the state's leading authority on yellow fever, was Mitchell's houseguest.

The two called on McCormick. He had great pain in his back, limbs, and stomach. His eyes had a faint yellow tinge. There was no black vomit. That was a good sign for the patient. Black vomit was the telltale symptom for patients likely to die. But it was obvious to the doctors that McCormick's intermittent fever was yellow fever. McCormick was quarantined.

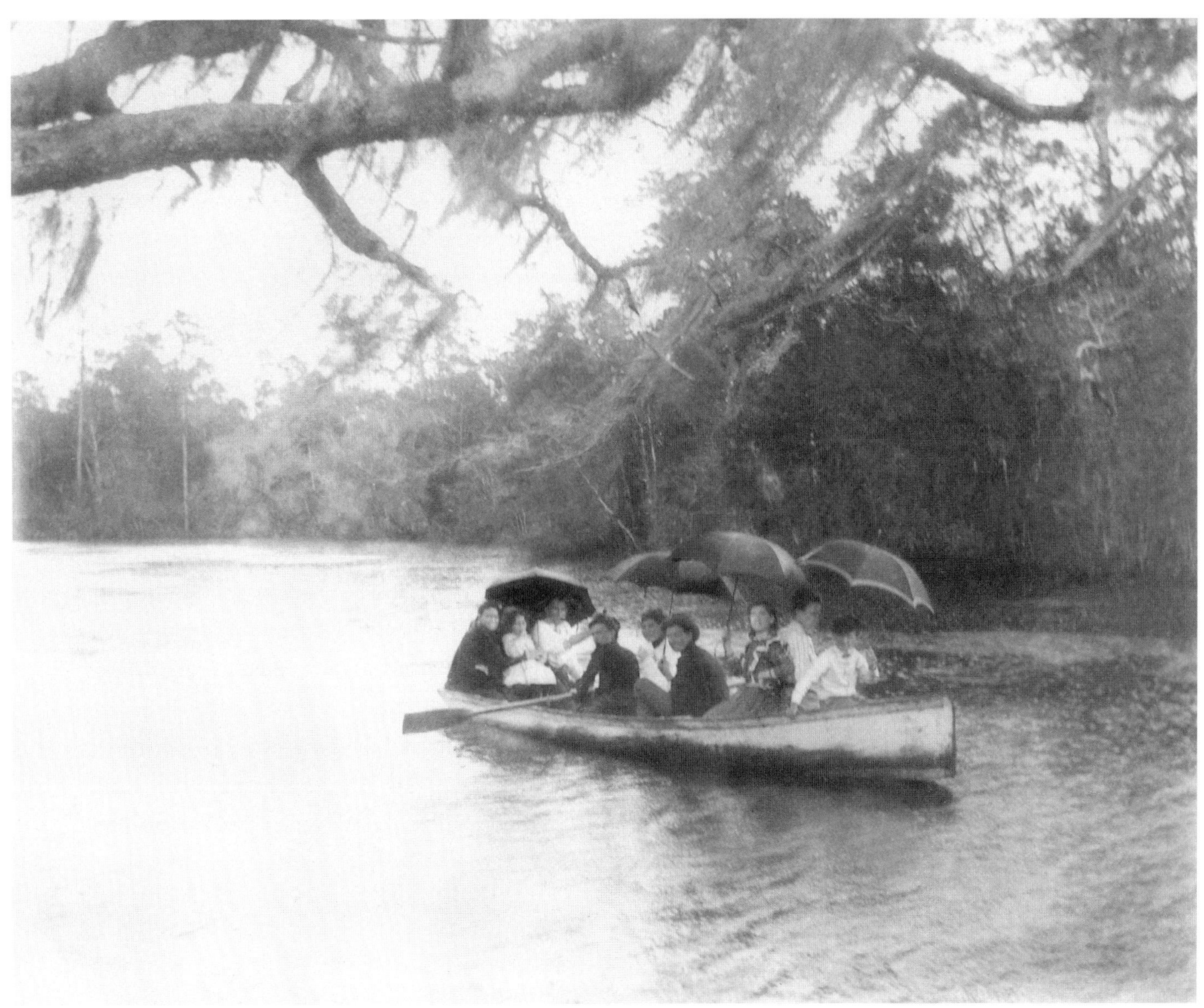

This boating party on Fishweir Creek came equipped for both sun and rain.

A week later, four new cases were discovered. These patients, as well as the Tampa barkeeper, were "official" sufferers of the dreaded fever. Now it was reasoned that several deaths from fevers of unknown origin earlier in the summer had likely been the result of yellow fever, isolated and unrecognized.

With recognition came fear, and no wonder—yellow fever ravaged a city, hitting all who lived there, even those spared the sickness. In August, an epidemic was declared, and people were not allowed to leave Jacksonville without either a medical pass stating that they had survived the disease and thus were immune, or a ten-day stay in a detention camp on the Georgia state line, near little Boulogne. After ten days, internees were given medical credentials guaranteeing that they were not carrying the dread disease.

The camp was hot, unsanitary, and inadequate. Jacksonville itself was hell. Before the epidemic ended in late November, one person in four—five thousand people in all—would be sick, and almost five hundred would die. It was, and remains, the worst disaster in Jacksonville history in loss of life.

The city tried to fight back, without success. Crews swabbed the city with disinfectant and stoked bonfires of pine and tar. On the off chance that concussion might kill the fever, cannons ringed the city and were fired often and regularly. The explosions reverberated like a doomsday clock chiming the terrible hours and days of the epidemic. Nothing worked, of course. The origin of yellow fever was not understood in 1888. Most people believed it was carried in the air, carried by the sick. Medical sleuths were getting close, but none had yet discovered that the culprit was the *Aedes aegypti* mosquito.

Perhaps Leah Cox looked back at Tallahassee and her family on the farm by the lakes and wished she had never left. Now, she could not return. People in Jacksonville might as well have been convicts or prisoners of war. The city was under siege by the fever and rimmed by hostile guards willing to tear up railroad tracks to keep at bay the people who might carry the fever.

Jacksonville had become a place of despair and ugliness.

A pall of smoke hung over the city almost from the beginning of the epidemic from the bonfires and the trash fires burned by thousands of households. Anything that might cause the fever was burned, including the clothing and bedding of anyone who was sick. Sometimes, fear drove residents to burn buildings where the sick had lived. There was talk of burning the Grand Union Hotel, where the McCormick family had stayed. Other guests on the register when the Tampa family checked in were quarantined for several weeks. After they left, the hotel was fumigated and boarded up.

The fires and the fumigations and the liberal use of disinfectants added a noxious odor to the smoke and summer heat. The stench itself was believed to be purifying.

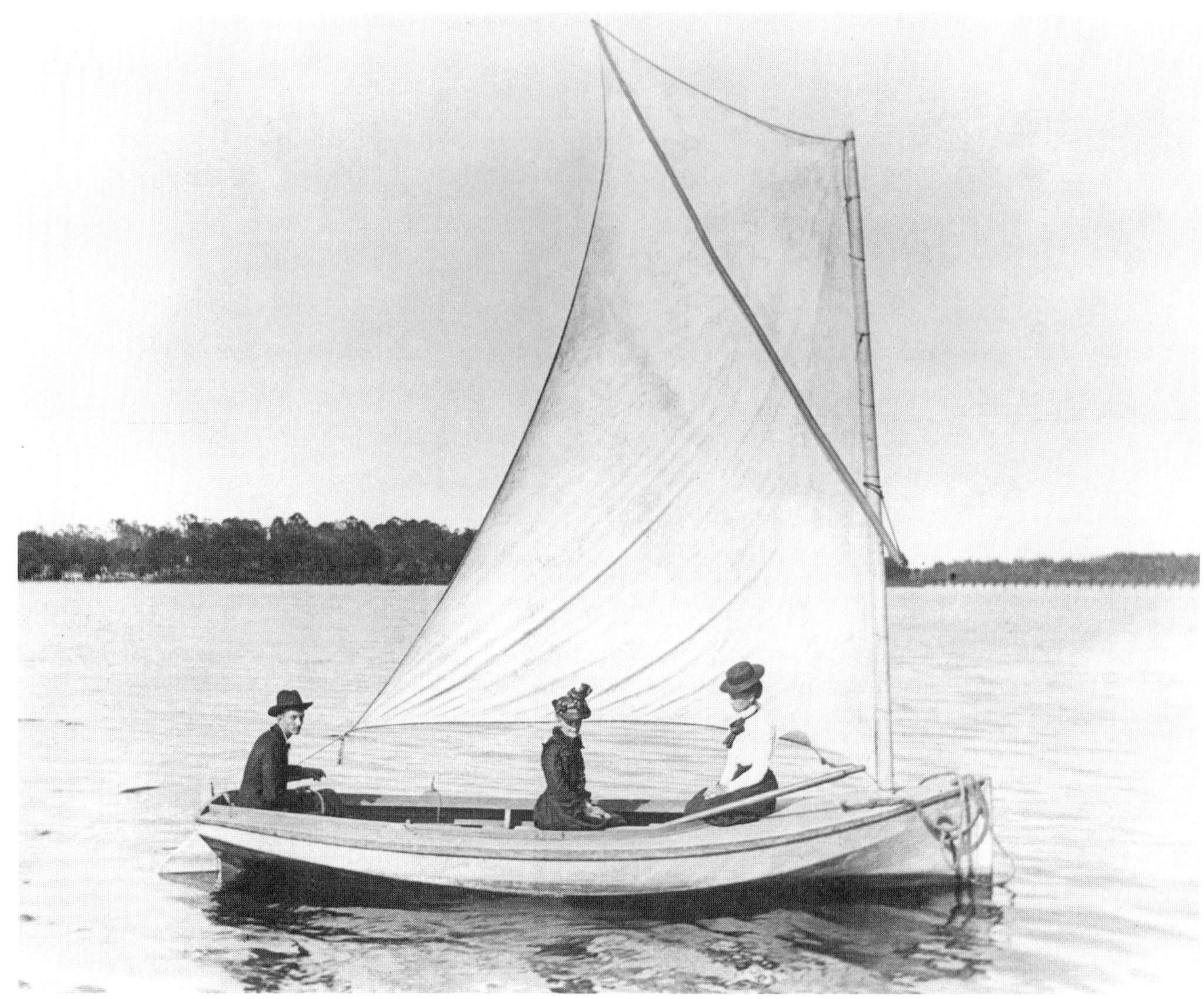

To catch this shot of friends sailing past, Cox and her camera stayed on the dock.

Predictably, the city suffered economic havoc from the epidemic. There was no trade with the outside world, no visitors arrived, businesses closed, and thousands of people were suddenly out of work.

Government of the city was taken over by the 282-member Jacksonville Auxiliary Sanitary Association, headed by Col. J. J. Daniel who, along with sixteen members of his group, died of the fever before it abated. Besides continual cleanup, the group, which met daily, set up emergency facilities to feed and house the hungry and homeless. Each week, the committee passed out food and necessities to the destitute—bacon, corn meal, flour, grits, molasses, coffee, sugar, a bar of soap.

The citizens were urged to keep to a diet of vegetables and plenty of coffee, no alcohol, little meat. Smoking was recommended. Staying indoors at night with windows closed or tightly curtained to keep out the night air was urged by the *Florida Times-Union* in its "Rules to Follow During the Prevalence of the Yellow Fever."

The newspaper had its own problems during the sickness. Nearby communities would not let it be circulated, despite its fumigation with sulfuric acid. The newspaper suspended publication on Mondays during the sickness because of the falloff in its revenues, plus difficulty obtaining newsprint and ink. And, over the course of the epidemic, the editor-in-chief, city editor, printers, compositors, and business manager all died of the fever.

The epidemic would not end until the first frost of 1888 came, on the day after Thanksgiving. In four months, yellow fever had devastated the city, scarring it permanently.

Leah Cox escaped the fever. But she did not escape the epidemic. It left her with a haunting sense of unfinished business, and it changed her life permanently.

During the months when travel from Jacksonville was forbidden, William Henry Cox, her father, died of the tubercular bone infection that had troubled him for years. Leah Cox could not go to her family to mourn for her father, a personal sorrow added to the sorrow of losing him. Barely launched on her bid for independence, she was suddenly, and for the rest of her life, the head of her family.

5

In later years, Leah Cox's nieces remembered her as a stern taskmaster. Is it any wonder? All of her life, she expected much of herself. Naturally, she required much of others.

Cox was twenty-one years old when her father died, leaving behind an invalid widow and the brood of Leah Cox's siblings—sister Esther, twenty, unable to work because of a rheumatic heart; sisters Lenah, thirteen, and Ellen, eleven; brothers Frank, fourteen, and Rowland, seven. Staggering as the change in her fortune and direction, Leah Cox did not shirk her responsibility. So far as we know, she did not even flinch from it. She took on a lifetime task of keeping her people together.

She did not have to do it, surely. She could have said: I cannot do this. I have no way to provide for a large family. I have no husband to help, not even an able-bodied brother or a strong sister to share the burden. I have no profession, barely a livelihood for myself as a beginning seamstress and apprentice milliner. But Cox did not look for a way out from under a burden many would have considered impossible to take on.

There is no way to know whether she ever doubted that she could keep her family together in an uncertain future. We can only know that she did it.

Her first goal after her father's death was to get the family together, to relocate everyone from Tallahassee to Jacksonville, quite an undertaking for a young woman with no money and uncertain prospects. One wonders why she did not return to Tallahassee; surely it would have been easier and cheaper, and there was the comfort of her uncle and aunt's family on the neighboring farm. But Tallahassee was not her choice, and, after some months, arrangements were made for the family to move to Jacksonville.

Cox's sisters Lenah and Ellen were to live with families from St. Andrew's parish. They would receive room and board and the opportunity to go to school in return for housekeeping chores. Brother Frank, who was retarded, was to do yard work for several families to bring in a little money. Brother Rowland, only seven years old, was out of the labor pool, along with the ailing Esther and the sickly mother, Ellen.

Lenah Geiger writes: "When the family arrived in Jacksonville, Leah had to carry, on her back, her 11-year-old sister who was ill with dengue fever, from the train station on Bay Street to East Jacksonville, a distance of about a mile."

The picture of a young woman carrying a sick child on her back through the streets is arresting. We can see it even though there is no photograph. Cox kept the image in her mind; otherwise, decades later, she would not have had it to pass on to her nieces and nephews, to make it part of the family's story.

If Leah Cox counted what it cost to become head of her family, not simply in pennies and dollars, but, more important, in terms of her personal life, we do not know it. But if she ran short of patience before her course was done, and we know that she did, it's no wonder.

She did not get to do what she had planned to do. She did not get to go where she had set her sights.

Years later, when she told the story of carrying little Ellen on her back to their new home in Jacksonville, was she saying, Look what I did for you? Or was she saying, Look at how hard things were? Both, perhaps. Certainly, both observations are true.

In the early months, Ellen, Esther, Leah, and Rowland shared rented rooms, but, before long, Leah Cox was able to rent a three-story house on Church Street. Everyone was together again. The big house was not an extravagance, however. It was a good investment. It could pay its own way. There were two apartments on the first floor, which were sublet. Rooms on the second floor were rented out. The Cox family lived in the attic, on the third floor.

These rooms were unfinished, but Leah Cox did not let that stop her. Lenah Geiger's memoir presents a picture of the young woman responsible for taking care of

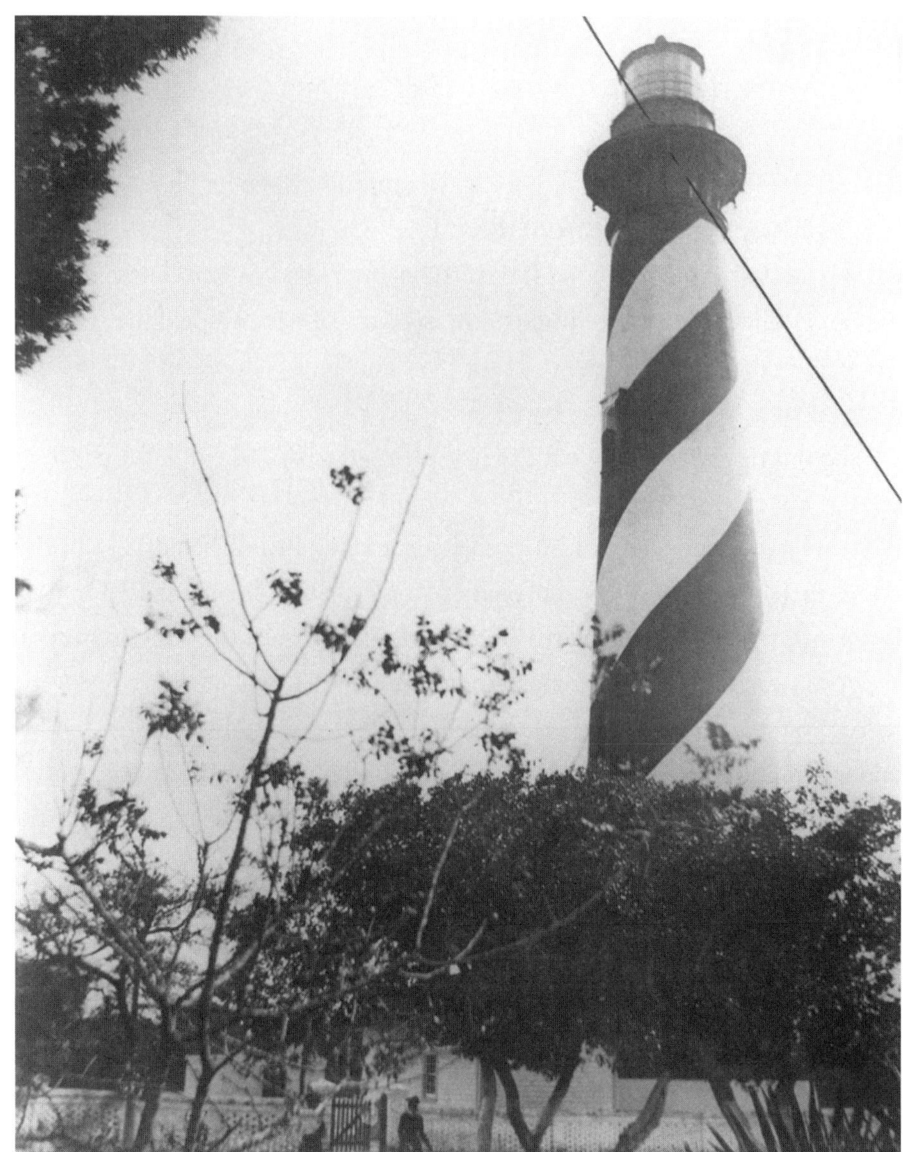

Leah Cox took along her camera to record visits to St. Augustine—the landmark lighthouse from the beach, and the beach from the top of the lighthouse.

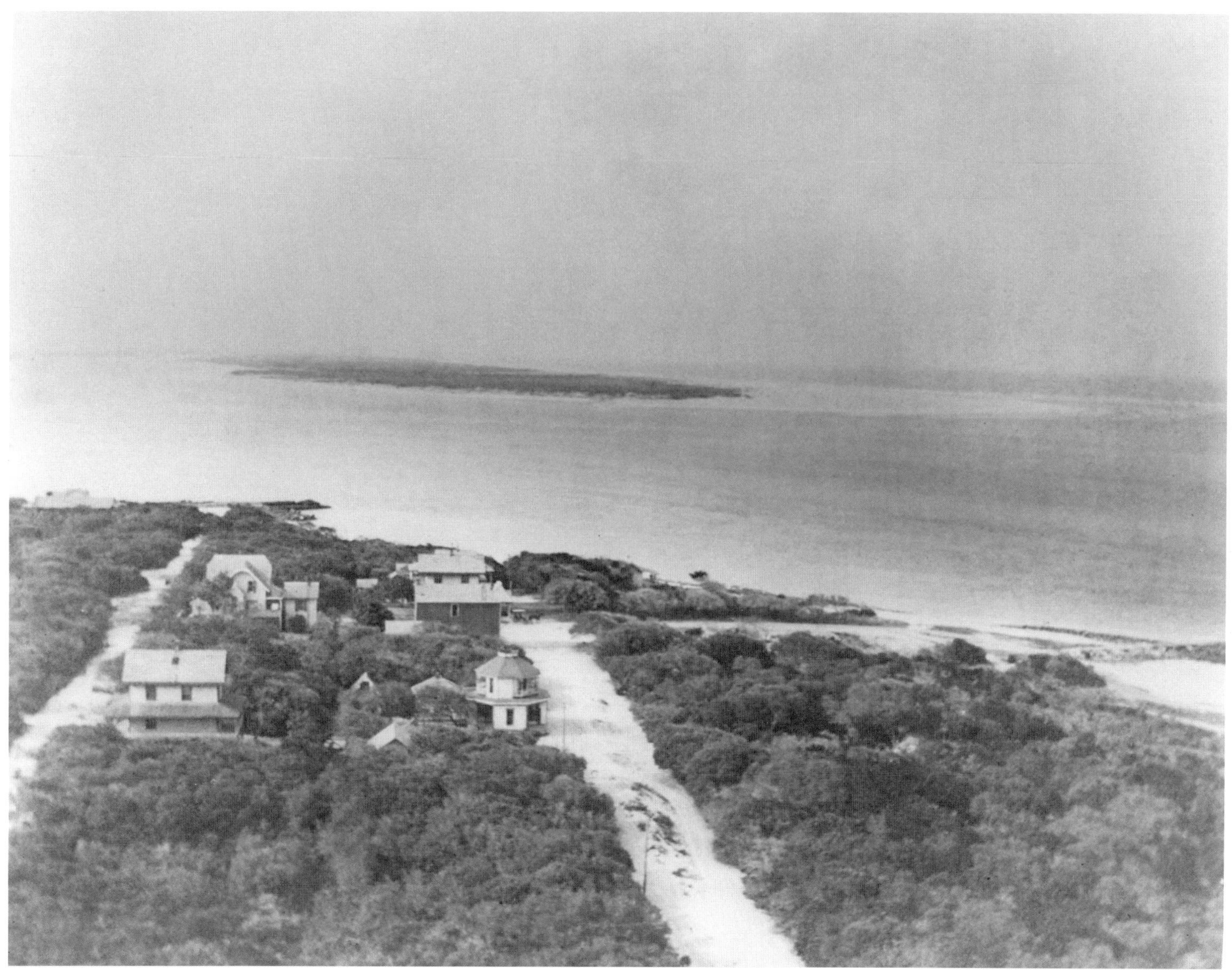

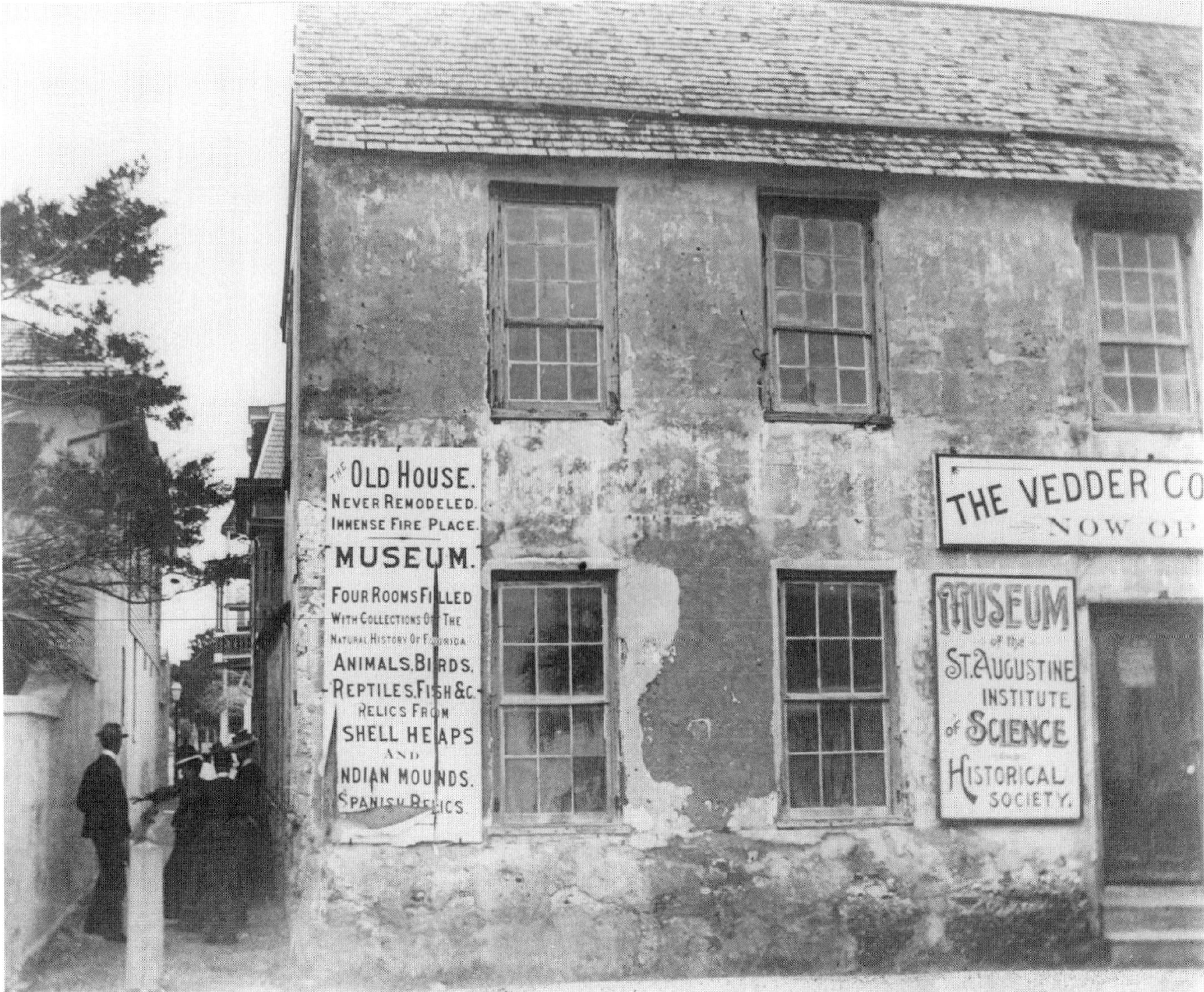

As today, in the early twentieth century the old city of St. Augustine promoted its antiquity as a primary tourist attraction. Cox documented the scabrous, "never remodeled" Old House that served as the Museum of the St. Augustine Institute of Science Historical Society.

a big house as well as a big family: "She became a jack of all trades, cleaning apartments and rooms, painting, doing repairs. She became very handy with the hammer and saw and other tools."

Cox could act as something of a guide, perhaps even a cheerleader, for her family as they began to explore the busy city, which moved steadily out of the shadow cast over it by the yellow fever epidemic. She had tasted the city full-fledged as a tourist and entertainment and commercial center before the epidemic, and she wanted it back. And she wanted her family to catch the spirit of the place too, to move beyond their loss and uprootedness into a sense of home, even in an unfinished attic.

Sometime in those last years of the century, Leah Cox acquired her camera. It was a large, unwieldy, professional-type box camera set on a tripod, built for manufactured gelatin-on-glass negatives. The manufacturing of negatives was a great step forward in photography. It freed photographers from the necessity of preparing and processing their negatives on site, immediately before and after use. These negatives came into use just after the Civil War, too late for the fairly numerous war photographers of the day to record combat scenes rather than the still images of smoking battlefields littered with dead who did not move and blur the picture, and of generals who posed studying their maps, and of soldier-comrades around the campfires on the eve of battle.

By the time Cox took up photography and it became for her a consuming avocation, her camera was something of a relic. By the end of the nineteenth century, the Eastman Kodak Company was already selling a simple, easy-to-use box camera preloaded with a roll of 100-exposure film. Much marketing was directed at women. The "Kodak Girl," introduced in the 1890s, appeared in ads as a fearless, globe-trotting young woman who kept up with the men—and got the picture, too.

But Cox didn't go the point-and-shoot route.

She was intrigued by a more complex and ultimately more rewarding piece of equipment. And, perhaps, she got a bargain. Florida Photographic View Company on West Bay street, which specialized in architectural photographs, photographs of land for sale, and other advertising illustrations, sometimes sold off used cameras when it bought new equipment. Cox may have spied the camera in the photography firm's window, surplus. How the camera came into her life is no longer known.

But Linus Scott, a retired engineer and university professor from Tampa who is Cox's nephew, remembers the camera. It is one of his few personal memories of his aunt. "I vaguely remember her having a big box camera—it was over a foot long and was ten inches by twelve inches. I remember a bellows on it, and a tripod."

Cox produced a large and diverse body of work with that camera. She did not often document great events, except perhaps for her photographs of the aftermath of the

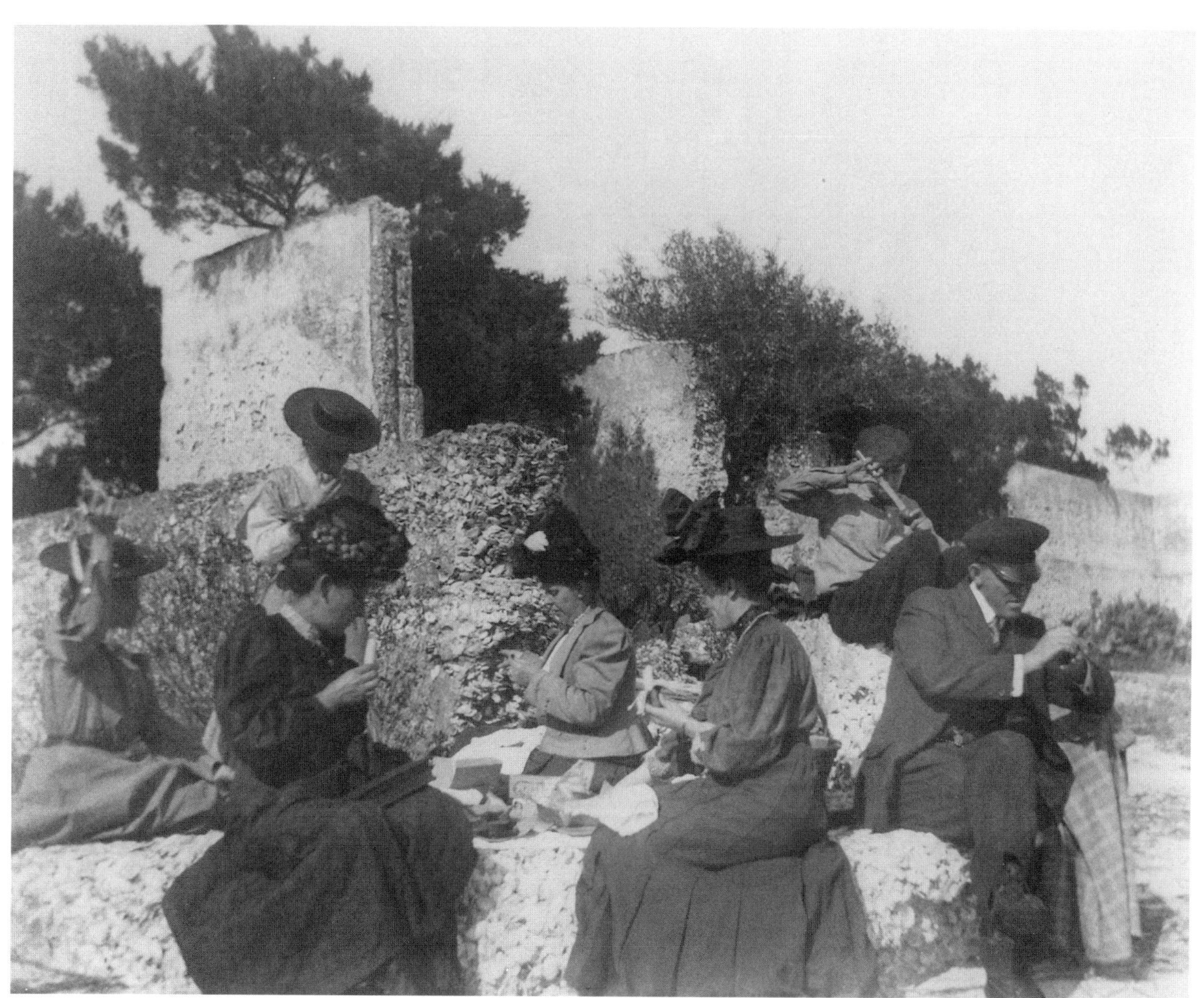

Friends picnicking on Ft. George Island, northeast of Jacksonville, opened their baskets in the ruins of a tabby-construction slave house.

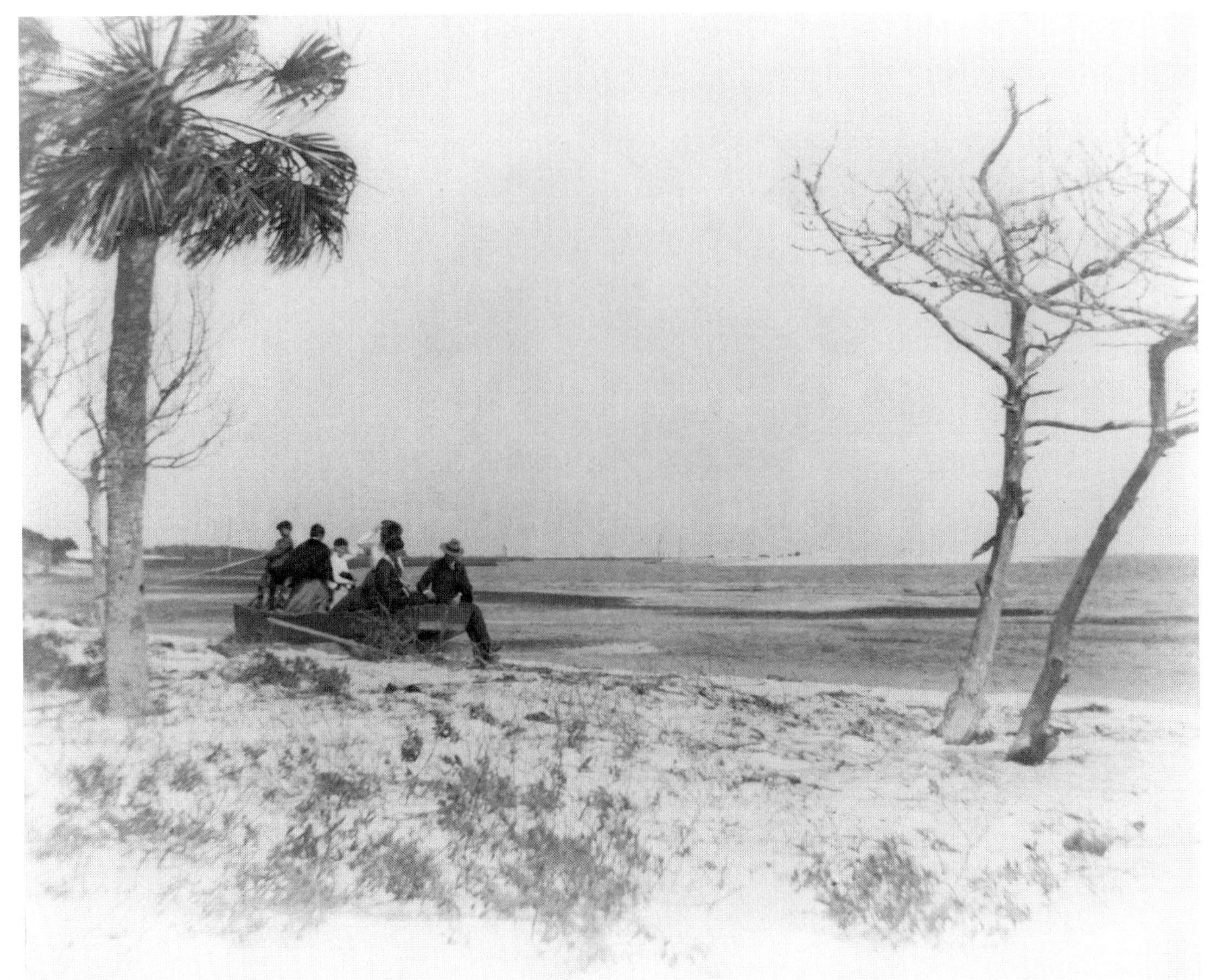

A party of picnickers at the beach of Ft. George Island. To the north, across Ft. George Inlet, is Little Talbot Island.

Jacksonville fire of 1901. Rather, she photographed places—buildings and cityscapes, the river and landscapes—and day-to-day events. She lugged along the big camera on outings to the beach and St. Augustine and Ft. George Island. The photographs might be called genre photographs, along the lines of the genre paintings of ordinary, secular, everyday subjects that began to appear early in the Renaissance and reached their zenith in seventeenth-century Holland—all those bunches of plump purple grapes and throttled hares in place of saints and martyrs. Leah photographed picnics and landmarks and recorded parish events. She had a knack for getting behind the scenes.

Jacksonville always loved a parade. On Labor Day and on the Fourth of July, citizens turned out by the thousands to cheer the bands and flags.

Another great parade each year marked Gala Week, a celebration tied to Thanksgiving. Marchers and carriages and a few automobiles were heaped with greenery and red, white, and blue streamers. Related to the celebration were golf tournaments, circus acts, horse races, and a football game between the Jacksonville Light Infantry and a team from Macon, Georgia. People came from all over Florida and Georgia for Gala Week. It was a bonus for tourists, a bonanza for merchants. In 1903, Gala Week was especially gala, to mark Jacksonville's recovery from the fire of 1901. It is easy to see Gala Week as a precursor to Jacksonville's annual Georgia/Florida weekend, right down to a football classic, and it must be assumed that the Cox family got involved.

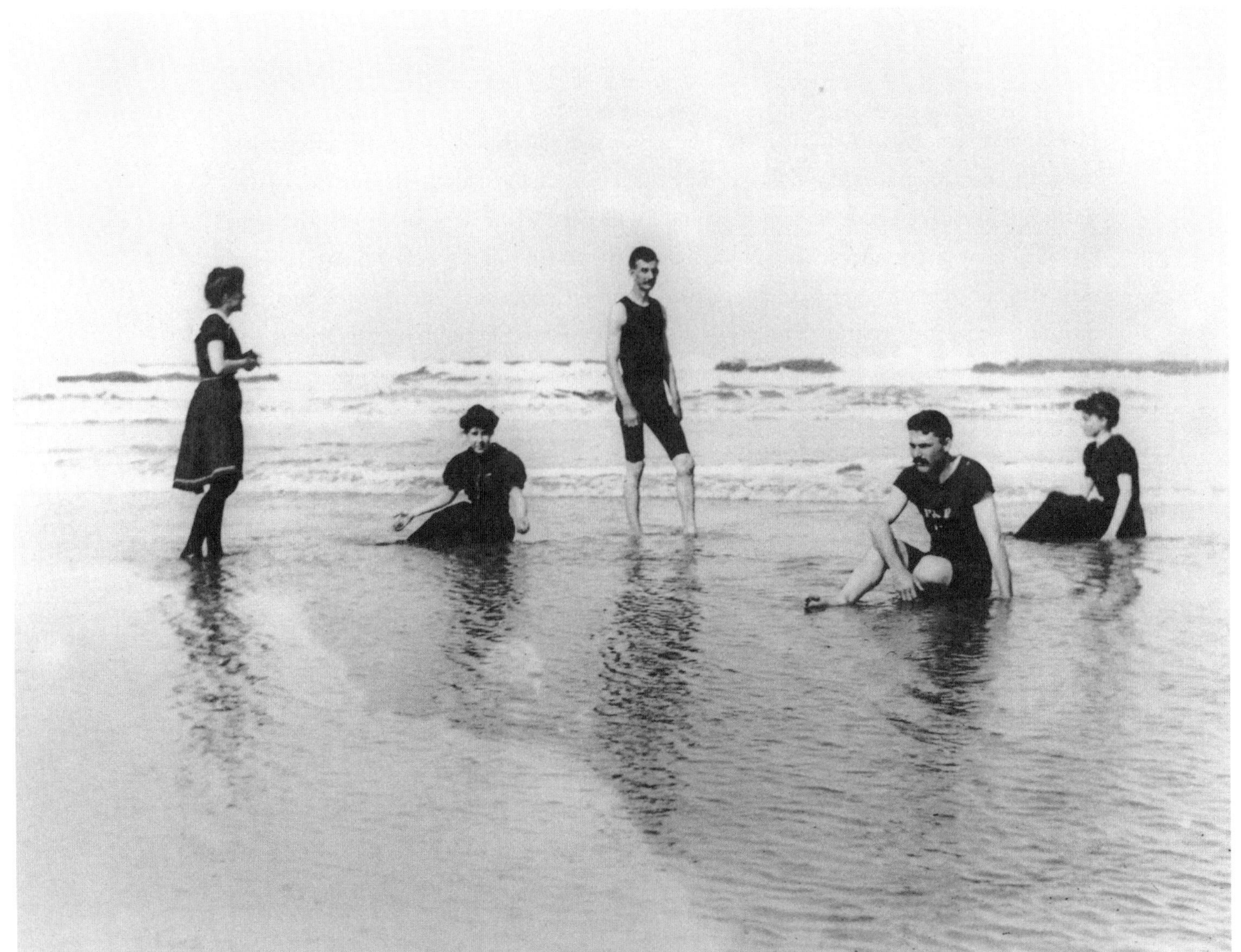

Florida's beaches drew plenty of fun seekers at the turn of the century, when Victorian mores allowed men but not women to show their bare knees.

There is an entertaining series of photographs among Cox's collection taken at the parade that celebrated the city's recovery from the 1901 fire. They show a time of transition. There are horses and buggies, automobiles not yet evolved beyond the horseless carriage. Folks are dressed in turn-of-the-century finery. And every lady and her attendant wears a hat, some of them, we can assume, turned out by Leah Cox, the milliner's apprentice, who had long since advanced to a full-fledged artisan of straw, felt, feathers, and flowers. Streets are wide and paved, streetcar tracks running down the center. Sidewalks are crowded, shops are hung with festive bunting. Flags fly everywhere. Marchers and riders move past the Windsor Hotel, where guests are stationed on balconies for a better look. Every buggy, every horse, every auto is decorated with a chain or two, or a mountain, of flowers.

Cox took many of these pictures as she wandered behind the scenes, snapping paraders getting ready to march. What is so clearly visible in these photographs of horses and buggies and people in their finery is the sense of community that existed in cities in the years before the First World War. There was a sense of pitching in, whether to fight yellow fever or to put on a parade. Everything we know about Cox says that she considered herself part of the team. Her photographs documented this.

At St. Andrew's, she took scores of pictures of the church and its parish hall and its people, the women of the auxiliary, the clergy, the choir, and acolytes. There are pho-

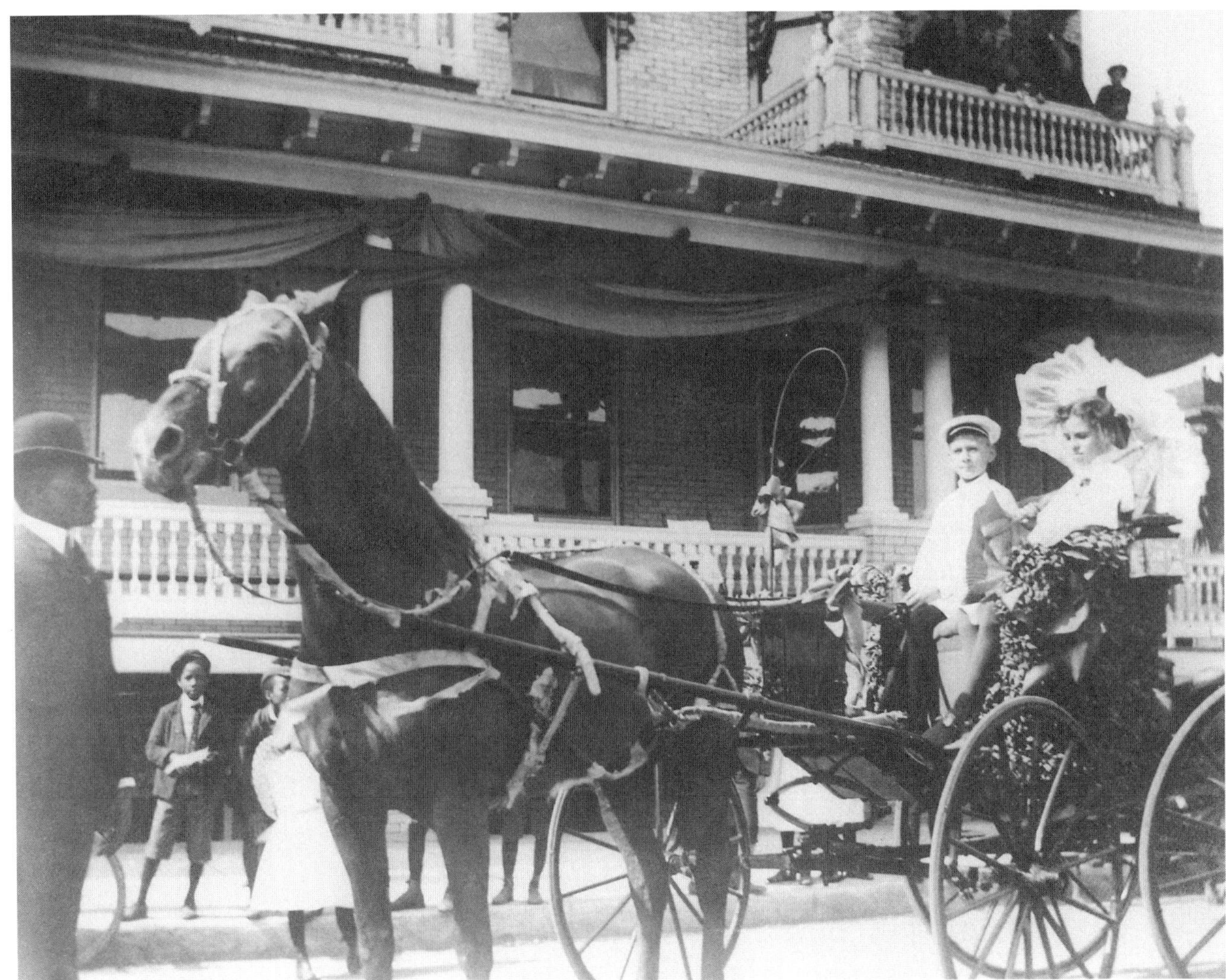

Gala Week in November 1903 took on special significance as a celebration of Jacksonville's rise from the ashes, from smoldering ruins to one of the nation's most up-to-date cities. An arch built over the parade route proclaimed, "The Gateway to Jacksonville."

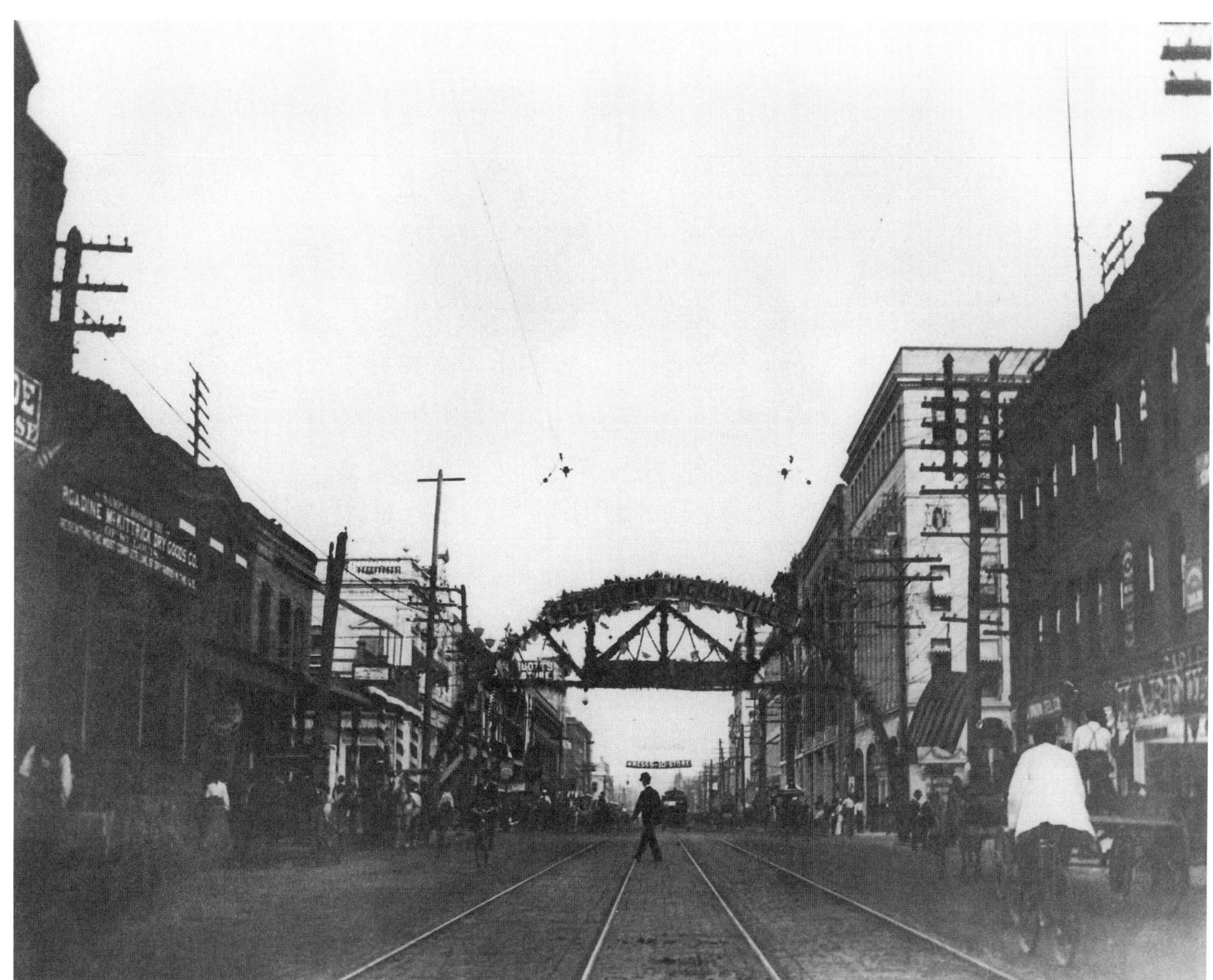
DRY GOODS CO.

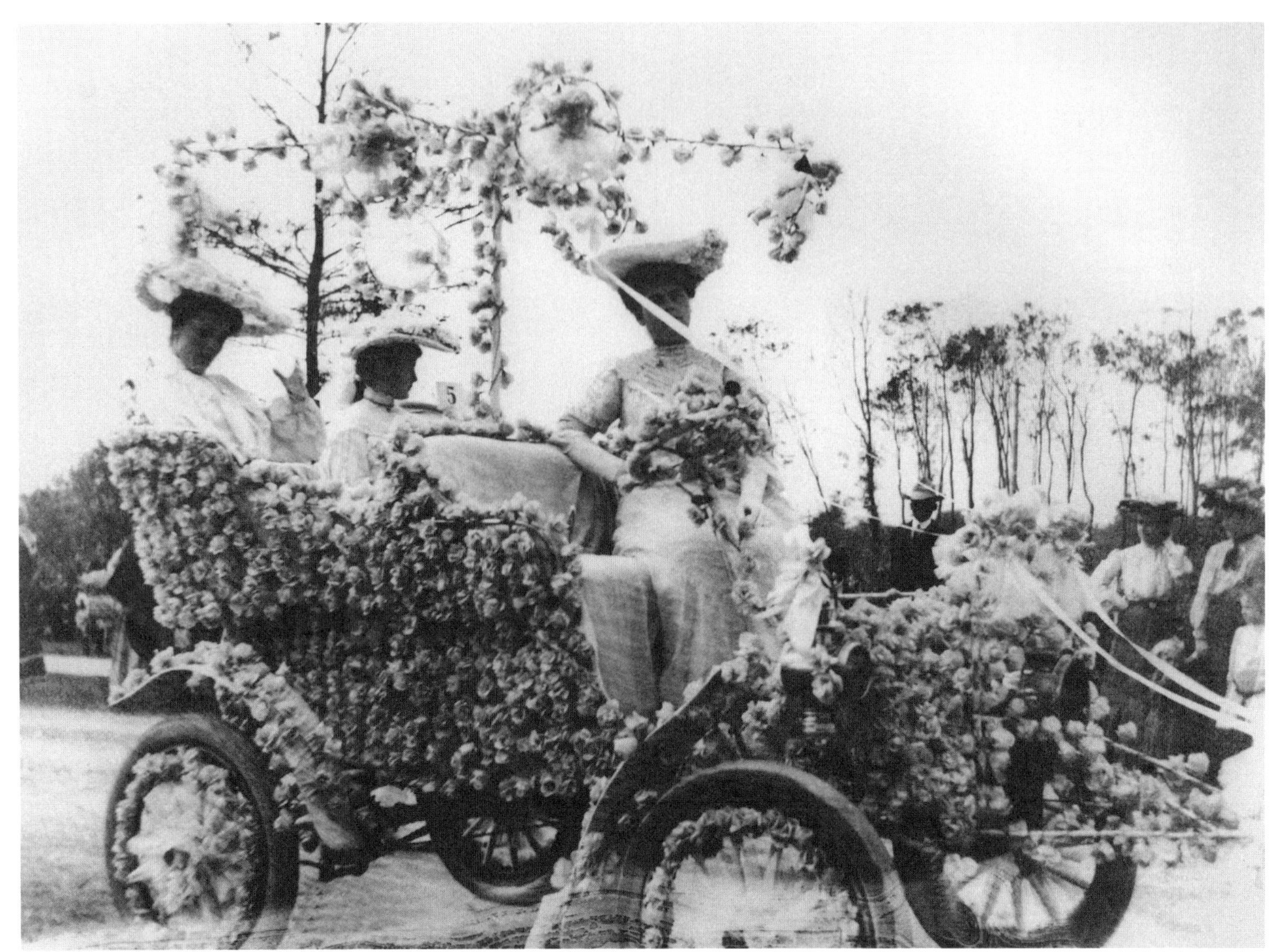

Flowers bedecked the horseless carriages and the ladies who rode in them in the Gala Week parade.

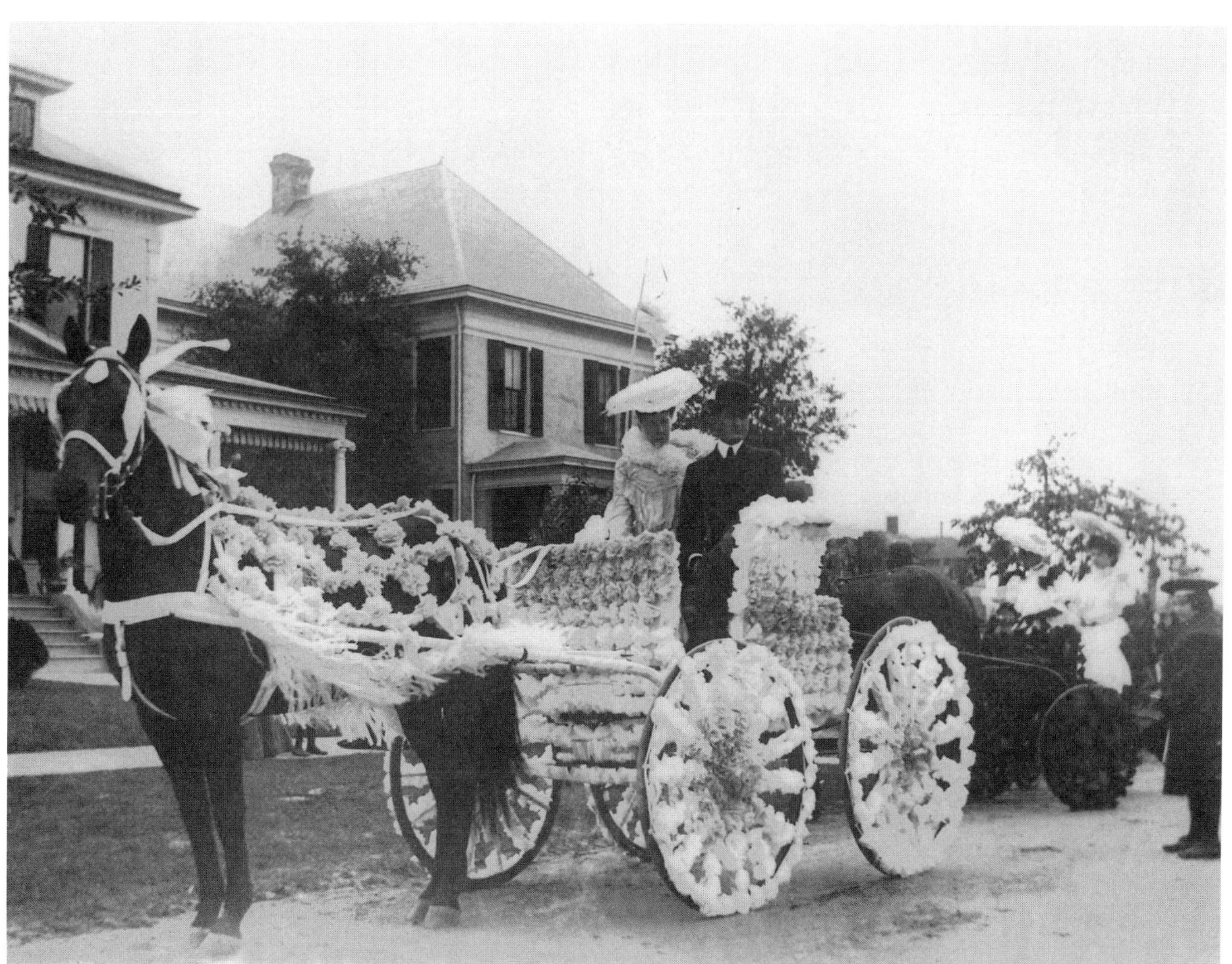

Frosted with flowers and streaming with ribbons, the horses, carriages, automobiles, parasols, and families in the colorful Gala Week parade celebrated the coming of Thanksgiving with a decorous competition.

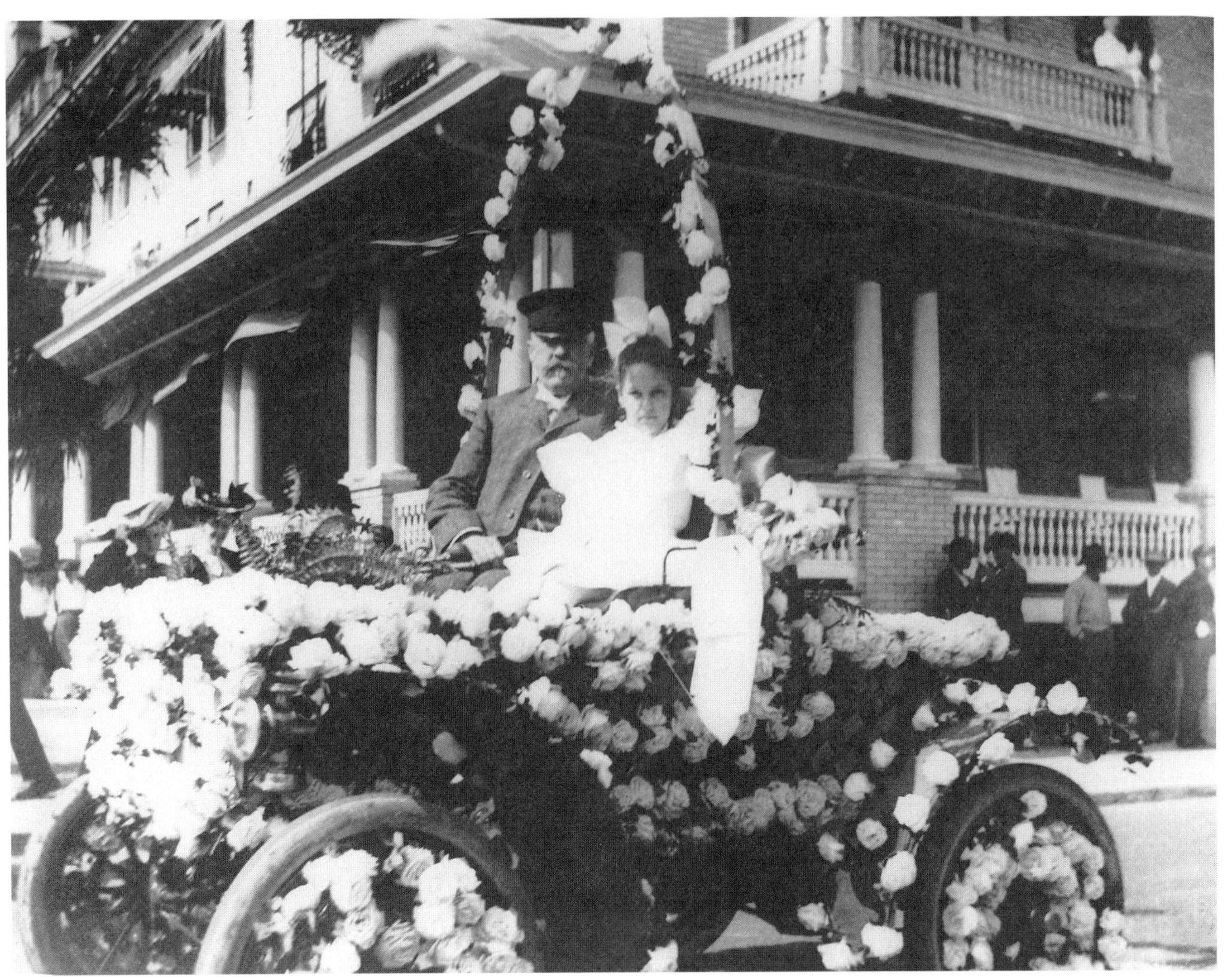

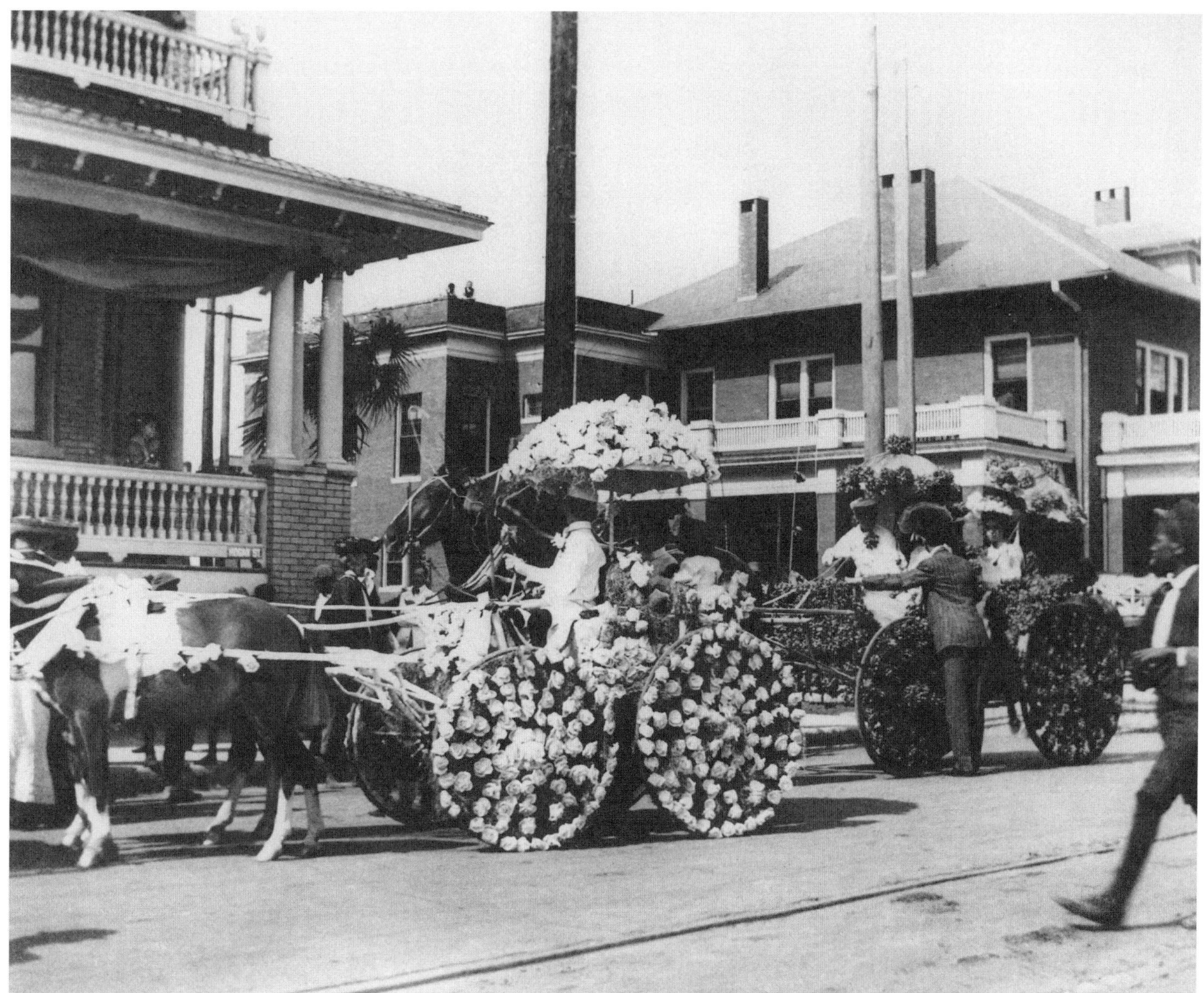

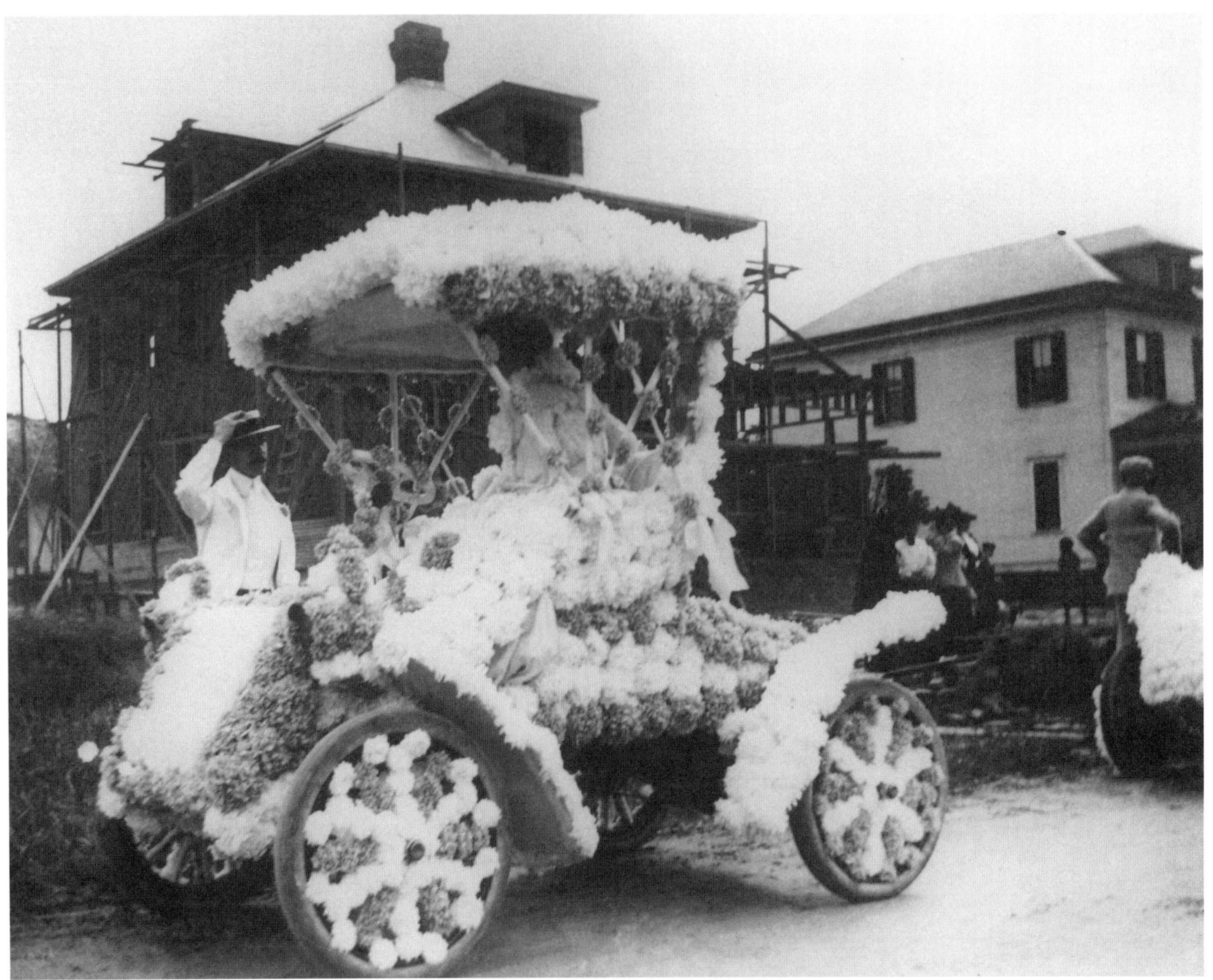

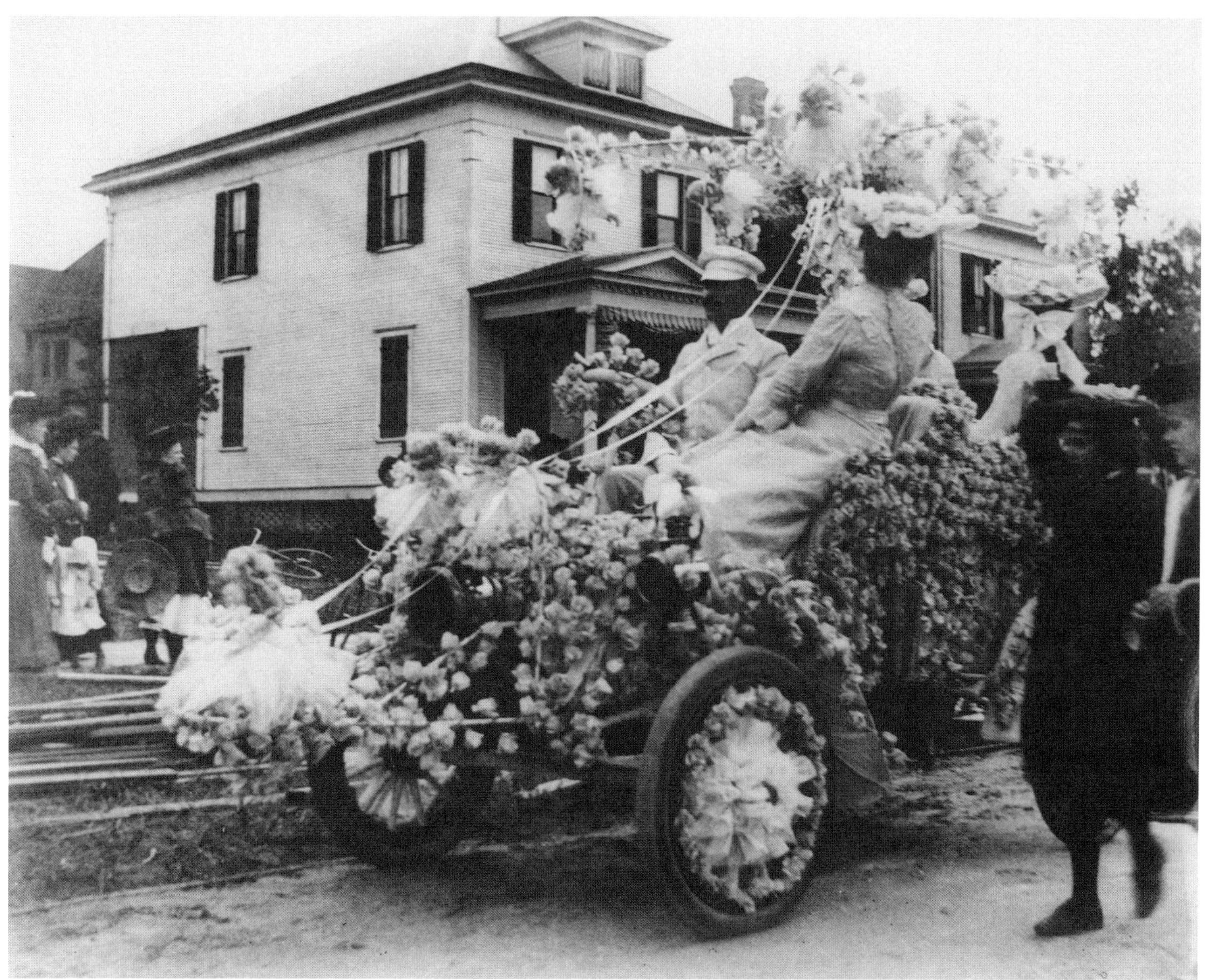

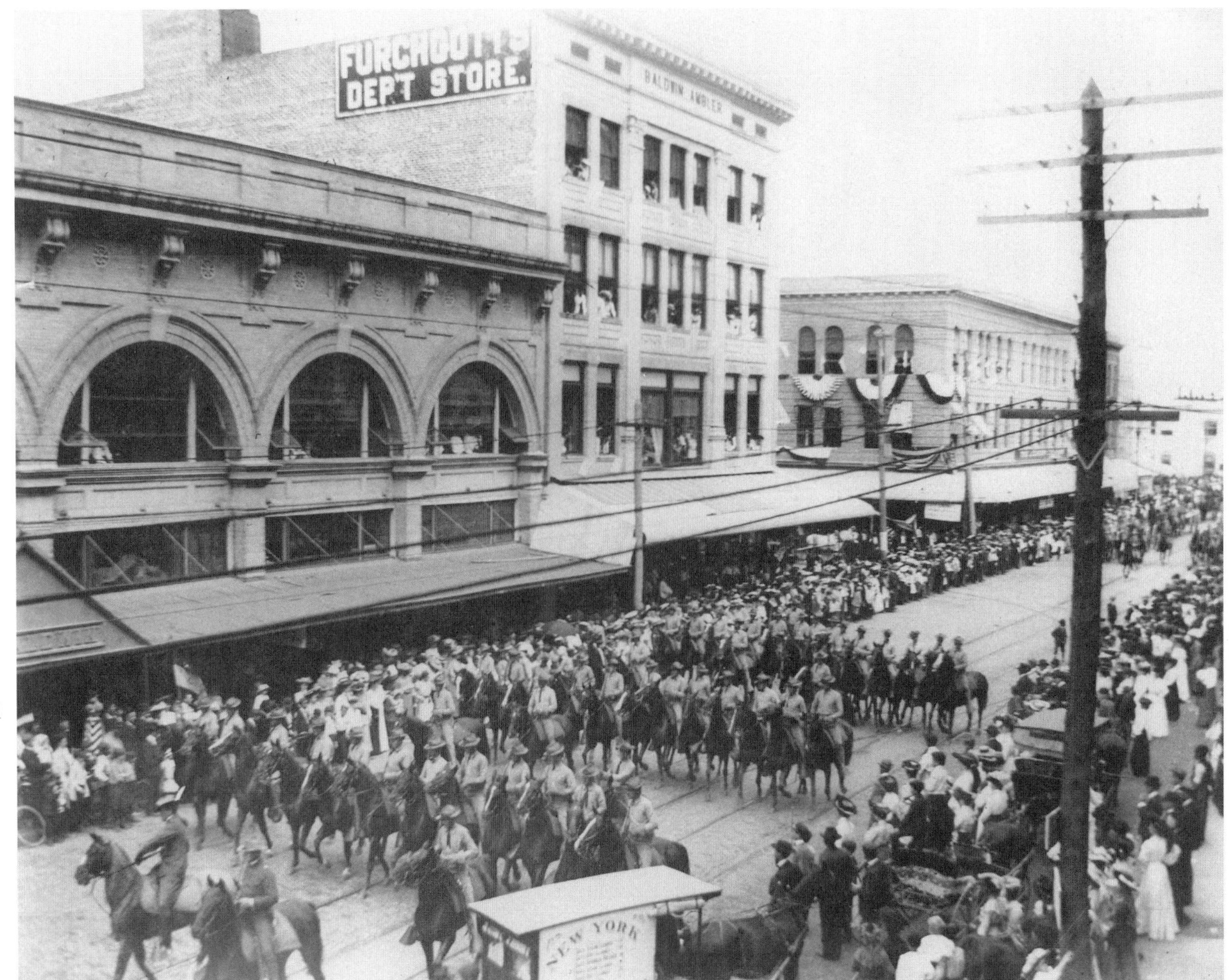

A company of troopers from the famous Seventh Cavalry rode in the parade. Department store owner Leopold Furchgott called Gala Week "the biggest time ever in Jacksonville."

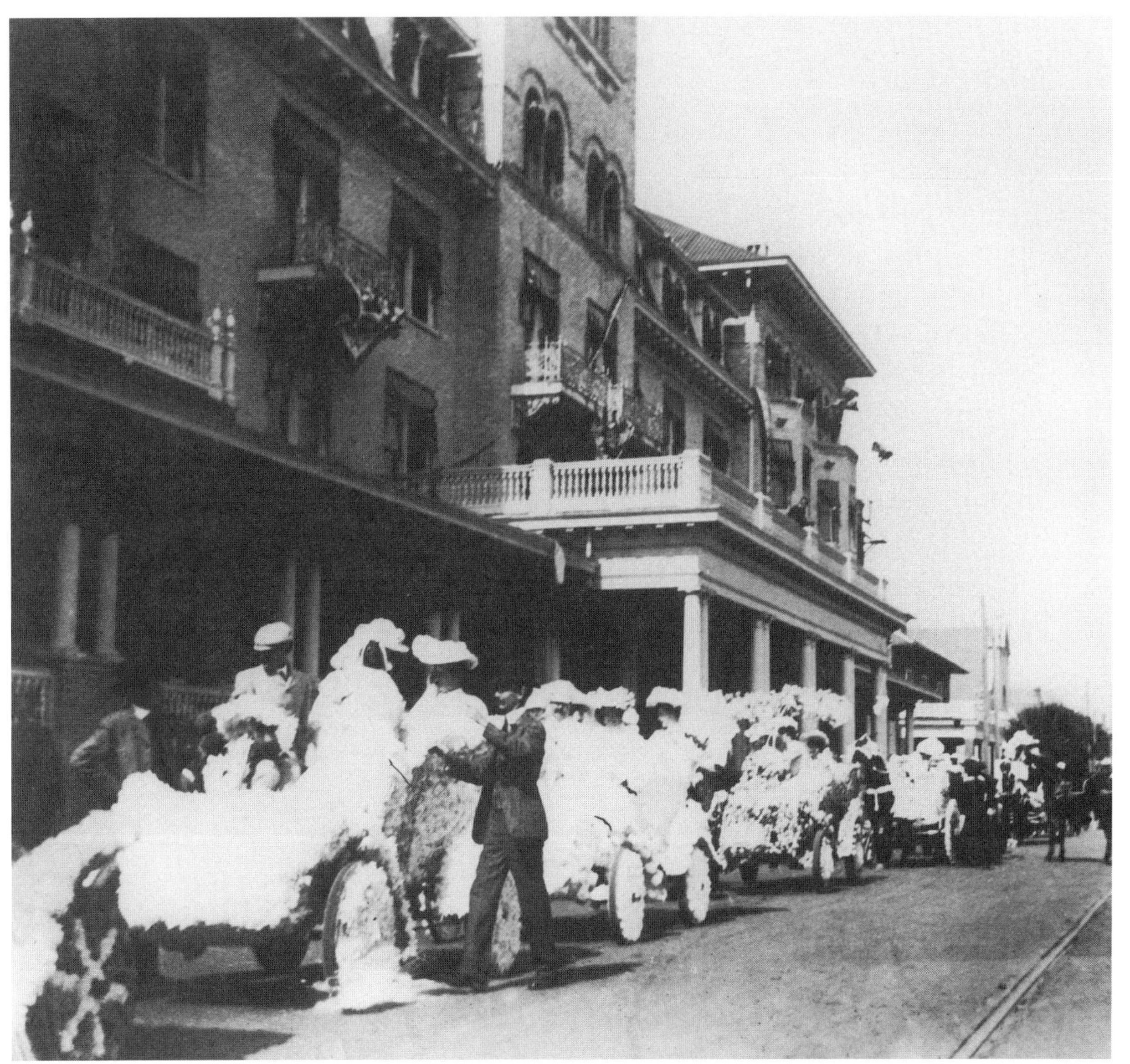

The richly decorated carriages taking part in the Gala Week parade lined up outside the rebuilt Windsor Hotel.

tographs of a parish bazaar the viewer can almost step into, to inspect the quilts and jams on display.

In fact, after the church was closed in 1957 by the Episcopal Diocese of Florida for lack of attendance and inevitably sank into disrepair, Cox's photographs helped resurrect it. When the church was restored to serve as headquarters of the Jacksonville Historical Society, her pictures were guides for the restorers.

Historical Society head Emily Lisska is certain that the restoration could not have been done so well, so authentically, without the Cox photos, many of which are now part of the society's archives.

Leah Cox's photographs of Florida's old capitol were also used by planners of the restoration of the building, when Florida built a skyscraper state capitol and restored the old building to an earlier edition to be used as a museum. Cox's photos, taken during a visit to Tallahassee to see family and friends, were valuable guides.

In the instances of St. Andrew's Church and the old capitol, Cox's work literally survives in stone because she was there to take the pictures—and because she took care of the pictures.

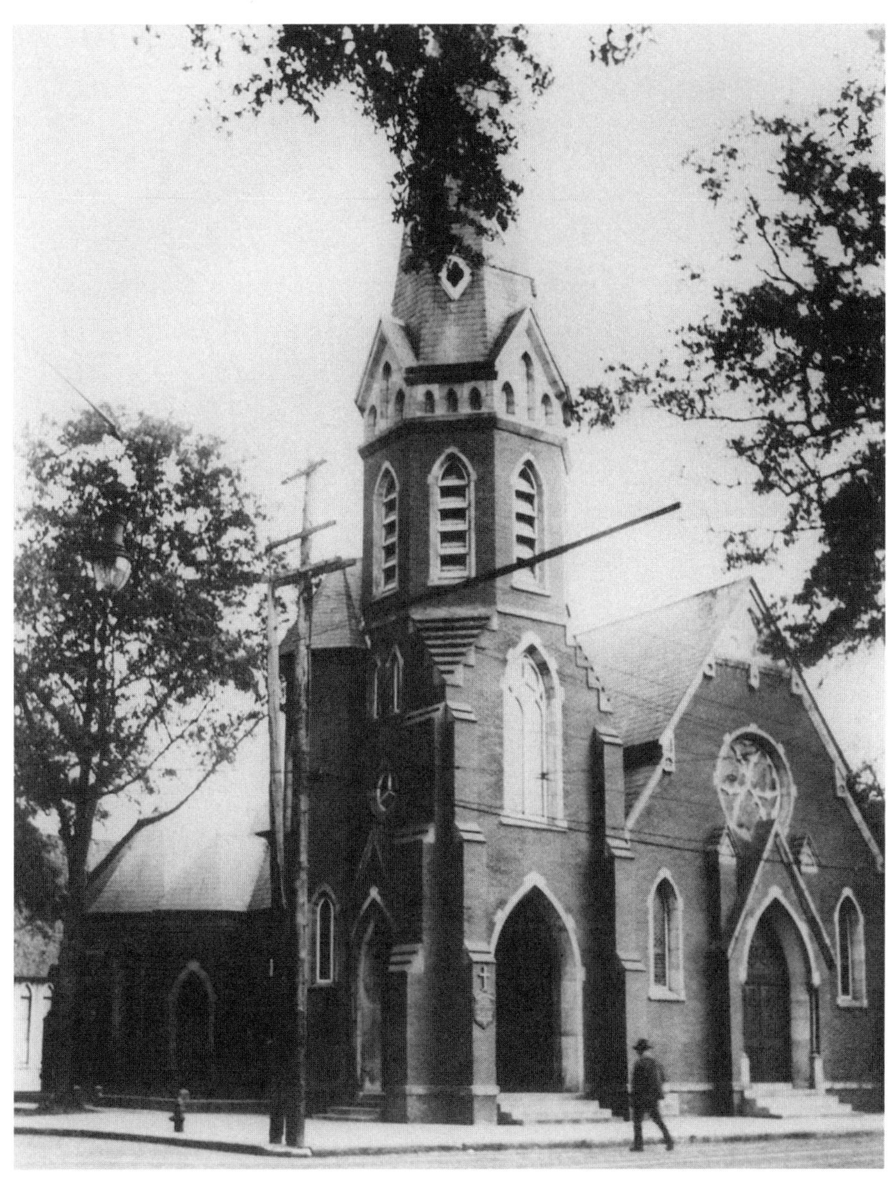

St. Andrew's Episcopal Church, now headquarters of the Jacksonville Historical Society, was Cox's parish all her life in Jacksonville. The first services in the church were held in 1888, the year that she moved to the city.

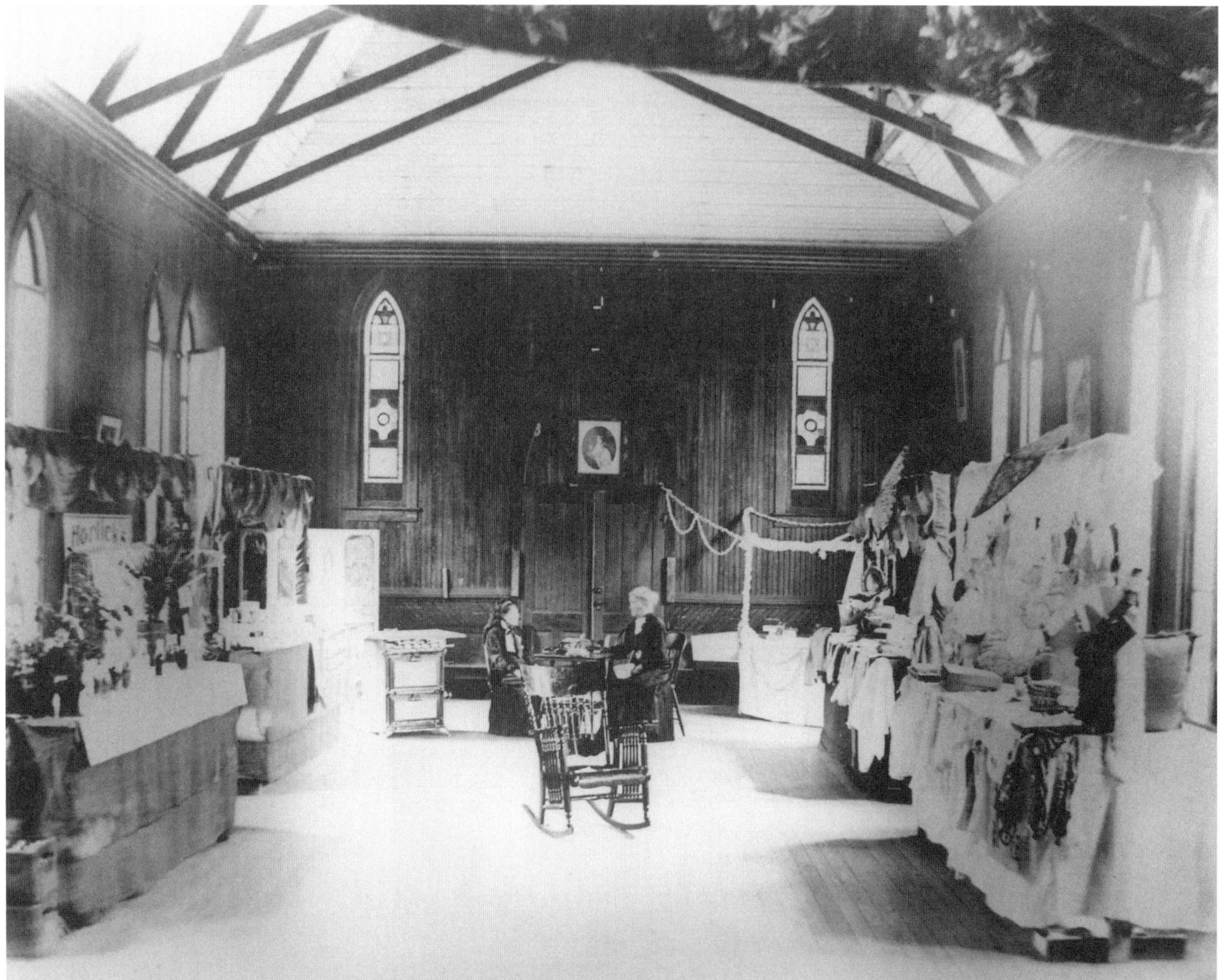

Cox documented every facet of parish life at St. Andrew's, including this church bazaar ready to open for business. As another contribution to the church, she helped build kneelers for the sanctuary.

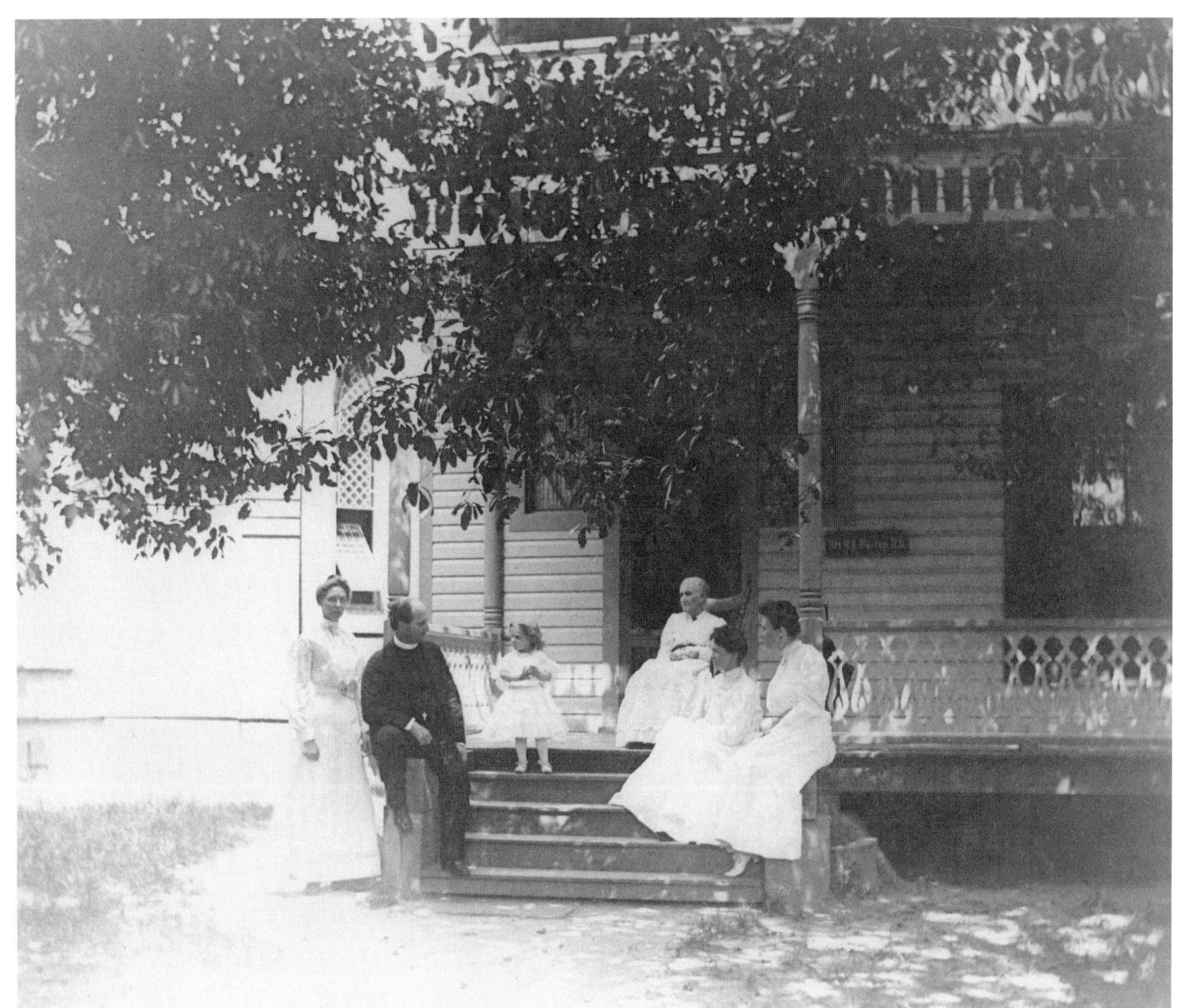

A St. Andrew's Church pastor and members of his family and flock relax on the shady porch of the rectory.

Laura Street ended in the St. Johns River, where on this day a sailing ship lay at anchor and a steamboat had tied up at the dock. A railroad trestle in the distance and horse-drawn wagons moving freight fill in this image of Jacksonville's modes of transport.

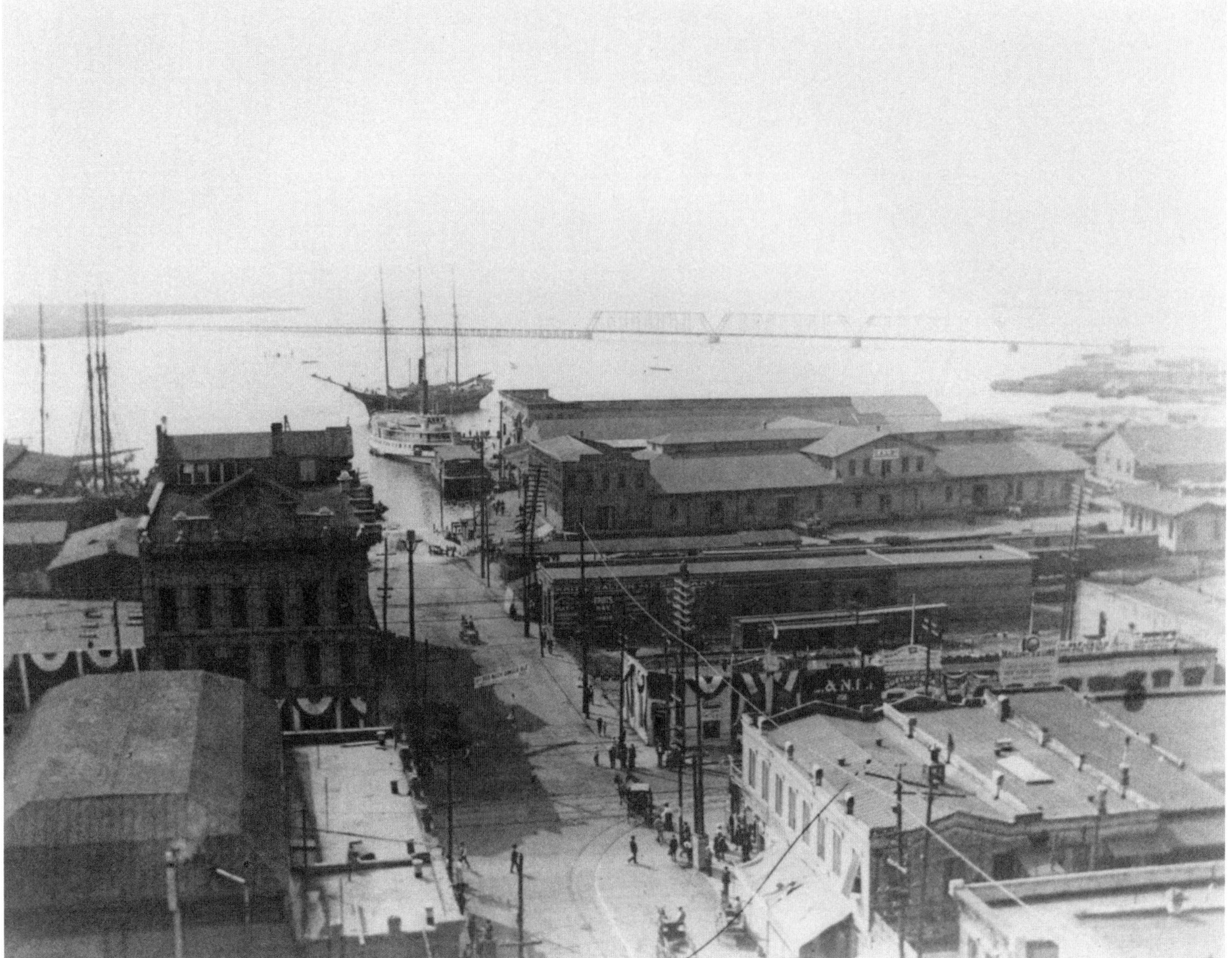

6

May 3, 1901.

The Great Fire, it was labeled while it still smoldered, and so it is called today, though it is long gone from living memory, retained as a civic history recitation without heat, without the urgent, unbelieving shock—and crazy, bounce-back optimism—of a city in ruins overnight and ten thousand homeless.

The most incredible and dramatic photographs of the fire were taken as the flames rampaged, seeming to pursue desperate men and women and children through the streets. Smoke billowed. Heat raged. People piled belongings into carts—or on their backs—and ran for their lives.

The city was caught in a firestorm. The smoke was visible—and interpreted as a city in flames—in Savannah, Georgia, and even in Raleigh, North Carolina.

Photographs of the fire in progress look like photographs of London in the Blitz during World War II. Photographs of the aftermath of the fire look like the surface-of-the-moon brick piles of photographs of post–Civil War Richmond, of post–World War II Berlin. About half of the city was destroyed.

We do not know where the Cox family spent the fire. It did not burn their home, separated by narrow Hogan's Creek from the conflagration. But the impact on the family, on all Jacksonville people, was enormous. People's jobs burned up along with their houses. Their clothes and dishes and furniture, stores of food, shoes, books, pianos, and treasures were lost. Some three hundred seamstresses were quickly put to work in tents pitched in Hemming Park to help with relief work, and it is natural to believe that Leah Cox would have been among them.

One of the city's newspapers, the *Metropolis*, called the fire "An Awful Visitation," and indeed it was. No picture could paint the horror, no pen describe it, the newspaper declared. But it was not for lack of trying.

When *Baltimore Morning Herald* reporter H. L. Mencken was sent to Jacksonville a week after the fire to cover the disaster, he learned that there wasn't a bed to be found in town—all were already occupied by newspaper reporters.

Leah Cox's most public photographs were of the aftermath of the fire.

Within a few days, less than a week, she was out shooting the city's charred bones. Two years after the fire, she returned to her vantage points to record the city growing back from the level ruin—houses and places of business, churches sprouting like the fresh, intense, iridescent grass of a forest floor that seems to come almost immediately after a wildfire, the grass that is greener on the other side of disaster. It was true of the city too. The builders set out from the beginning to build a modern, up-to-code city on the ashes of the old Jacksonville. And no time was wasted. In a day, the cleanup had begun, and in a week, Jacksonville was fully involved in the work of recovery and rebuilding. Help promised from across the country began to roll in. Indeed, part of Mencken's assignment was to trace two carloads of supplies—including coffins and whiskey—sent from Baltimore.

The Jacksonville fire was the largest metropolitan fire ever to occur in the South. One of its major casualties was the business of government. All public buildings lay in ruins; most of the city's records were destroyed. It was promising ground for chaos, but chaos did not take root.

A commission of public-minded citizens—much like the group that had formed during the yellow fever crisis—was quickly in place. Citizens' committees to oversee relief, sanitation and public health, housing, employment, transportation, and the keeping of order were established immediately.

Cox began to prowl the city to record its first days of recovery. There are no photographs of the fire itself in her collection, or of the immediate, dangerous aftermath when debris smoldered, blocking streets, and militia patrolled. Within a week, however, workers had cleared much debris; they had pulled down killed trees and broken utility poles. Streets were narrow, swept-clean lines marking a grid in the ashes. Along them, the ashes sprouted solitary, sentinel chimneys and a few naked, blackened trees left standing in the hope that there could yet be life in the roots.

One might have met Cox roaming that wasteland, toting her unwieldy box camera, climbing to the roofs of structures left standing to get the best point of view, recording the amazing devastation. A photographer is motivated by the conviction that there is something that needs saving. This awful visitation needed saving.

It began so insignificantly. Who would have believed that a few sparks could burn down a city? The fire was started by a spark from a noonday cook fire in a shanty near the Cleveland Fiber Factory at Beaver and Davis Streets. The spark fell on racks of drying Spanish moss. Workers on their noonday break noticed smoke and tried to put out the fire, but it hung on, stubborn and hungry. The moss flared and ignited a storage shed packed with more dry moss, The air was dry. The wood was dry. Too quickly, the shack exploded into flames, and when the shed roof collapsed, burning moss was carried away on a fresh northwest wind. Drifting incendiary bundles settled back to earth, setting half the city on fire.

The fire was uncontrollable virtually from the beginning. There were drought conditions. The fire agitated a breeze into a fitful, unpredictable wind. In hours, firefighters were in Jacksonville from as far away as Savannah, which sent a special trainload south. But there was no way for 1901 equipment to handle the fire. Buildings exploded with heat build-up; people fleeing the fire who dropped their goods, thinking they would be safe, looked over their shoulders to see their bundles in flames. Huge piles of household goods left in Hemming Park were mounds of ash when their owners returned.

The fire took at least seven lives. It gulped up $15 million in property—2,368 shops, homes, office buildings; 10 hotels; 23 churches. Most of downtown was simply gone after the fire's eight-hour rage, which ended when the wind dropped and a light rain fell in the early evening.

Immediately, like combat veterans reliving a battle, Jacksonville folk began telling each other tales of survival and its aftermath.

A little girl put aboard the riverboat *May Garner* with her invalid aunt to escape the fire recalled the docks burned to the river's edge, recalled that the boat could not approach the shore because of the floating debris and logs.

"I shall never forget the hissing of the big logs as they floated by or the bundles of ignited fiber as they were carried by the strong west wind through the air above the flaming city," recalled Linda Rebekah Frost Sheddan, ten years old at the time of the fire, when she wrote an account of her adventures years later reported in the *Florida Times-Union*.

The steamboat *May Garner* could not be brought to shore in the flaming, chaotic

The Windsor, the only tourist hotel rebuilt on a grand scale after the Great Fire of 1901, covered a full block west of Hemming Park. These two views of the hotel show the main entrance, which faced the park, and the north side of the building, where construction progressed at a slower pace. In that photo, a new house has risen in a block that remains to be rebuilt. The tent at the corner of the lot operated as a commercial location.

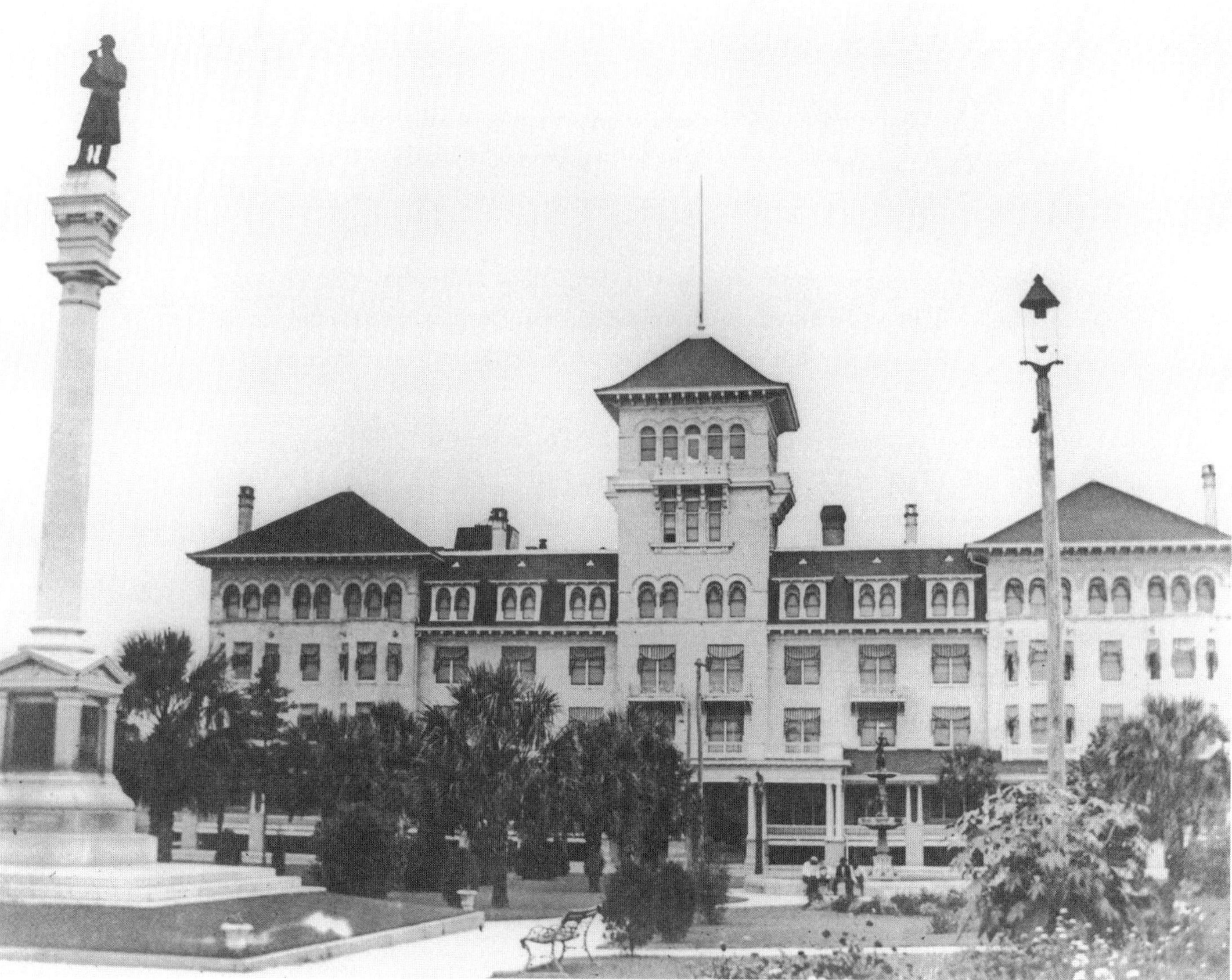

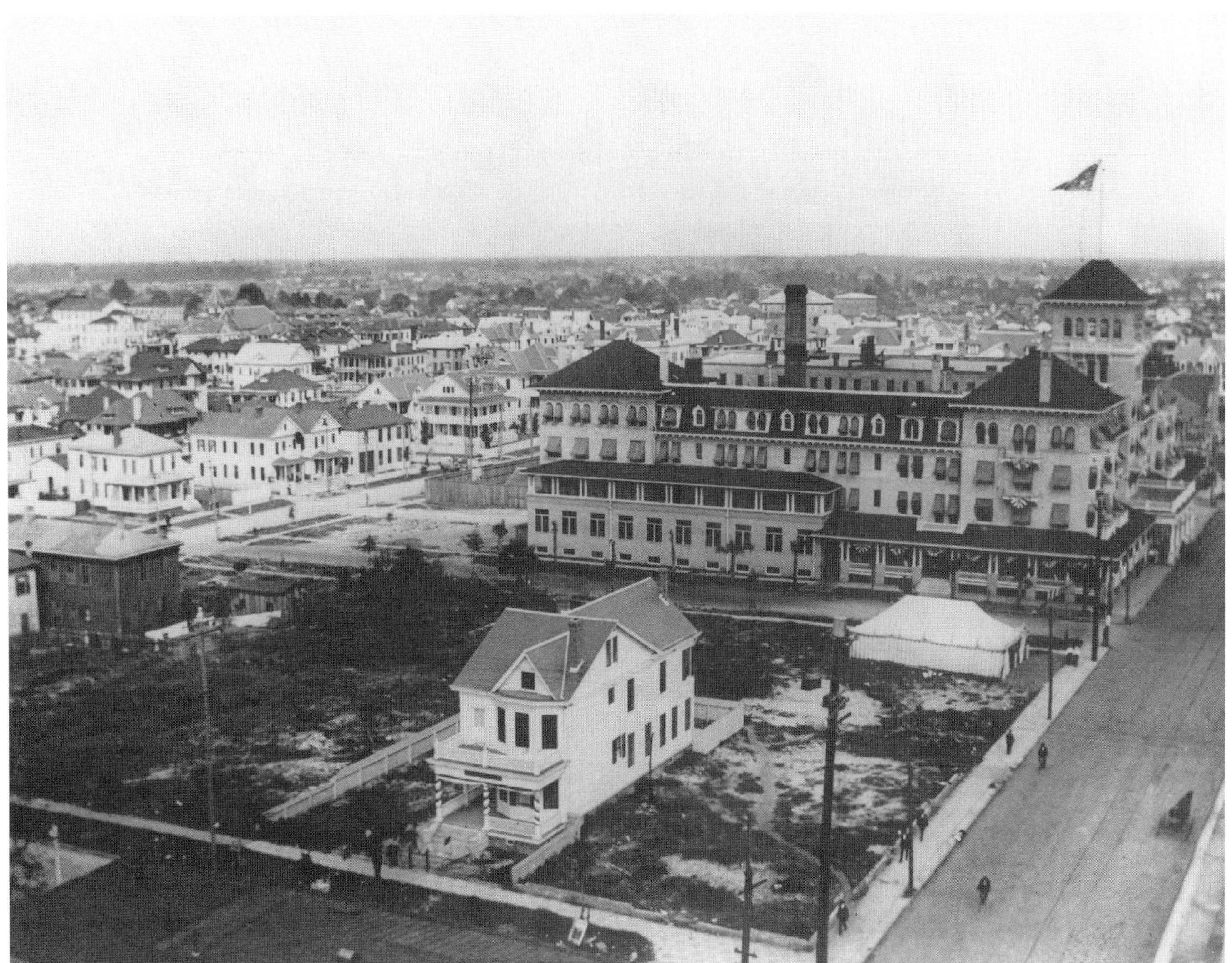

downtown area. The captain finally tied up at a private dock just west of the city in the Riverside area, and the child and her aunt made their way to the house of a family friend. Never mind that Linda Rebekah was finally safe from the fire, she became determined to find her mother. She scouted the long driveway that led from the house to Riverside Avenue. The gate was not locked. She took off running.

Soon she was in unknown territory. She began to search for her mother in the smoldering ruins.

> *I came to where the trees had shriveled and curled up. Another block on the avenue, and the trees had no leaves; another block and there were no trees, or flowers, or shrubbery. Only black skeletons that had once been trees could be seen. . . .*
>
> *The ashes under my feet were hot. My Roman sandals were burning my feet and I was a sight. My white dotted Swiss dress was mussed and dirty. I had to stop and catch my breath. . . . No one was anywhere. I was alone in a sea of dust and ashes. I had not seen a single human being the whole time since I left that house in Riverside.*

Later, the child stopped at the ruins of the Church of the Immaculate Conception to catch her breath, to search for a landmark that might point her home.

> *At last I came to a wall still standing, the front wall of a church, but that was all. The*

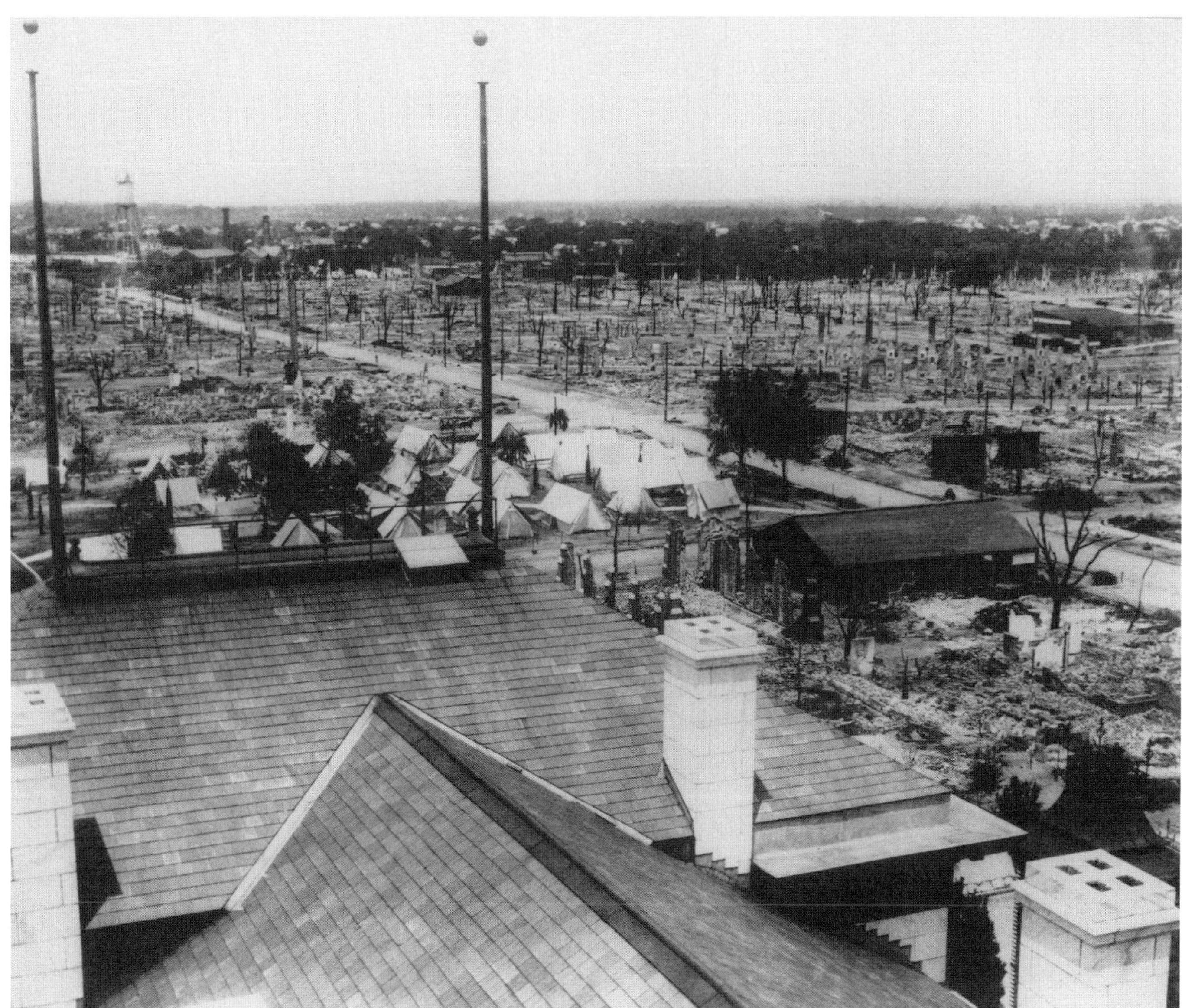

In 1901 Leah Cox set up her camera on the roof of the Federal Building to photograph the devastation of the Great Fire. The tent city pitched in Hemming Park provided temporary shelter for those left homeless by the fire, as well as space for emergency services.

In 1903, Cox returned to the Federal Building to record two years' worth of progress. Flags now fly from the twin poles, the tents are gone from the park, and a new crop of houses has sprung up where only burned power poles stood in the days after the fire.

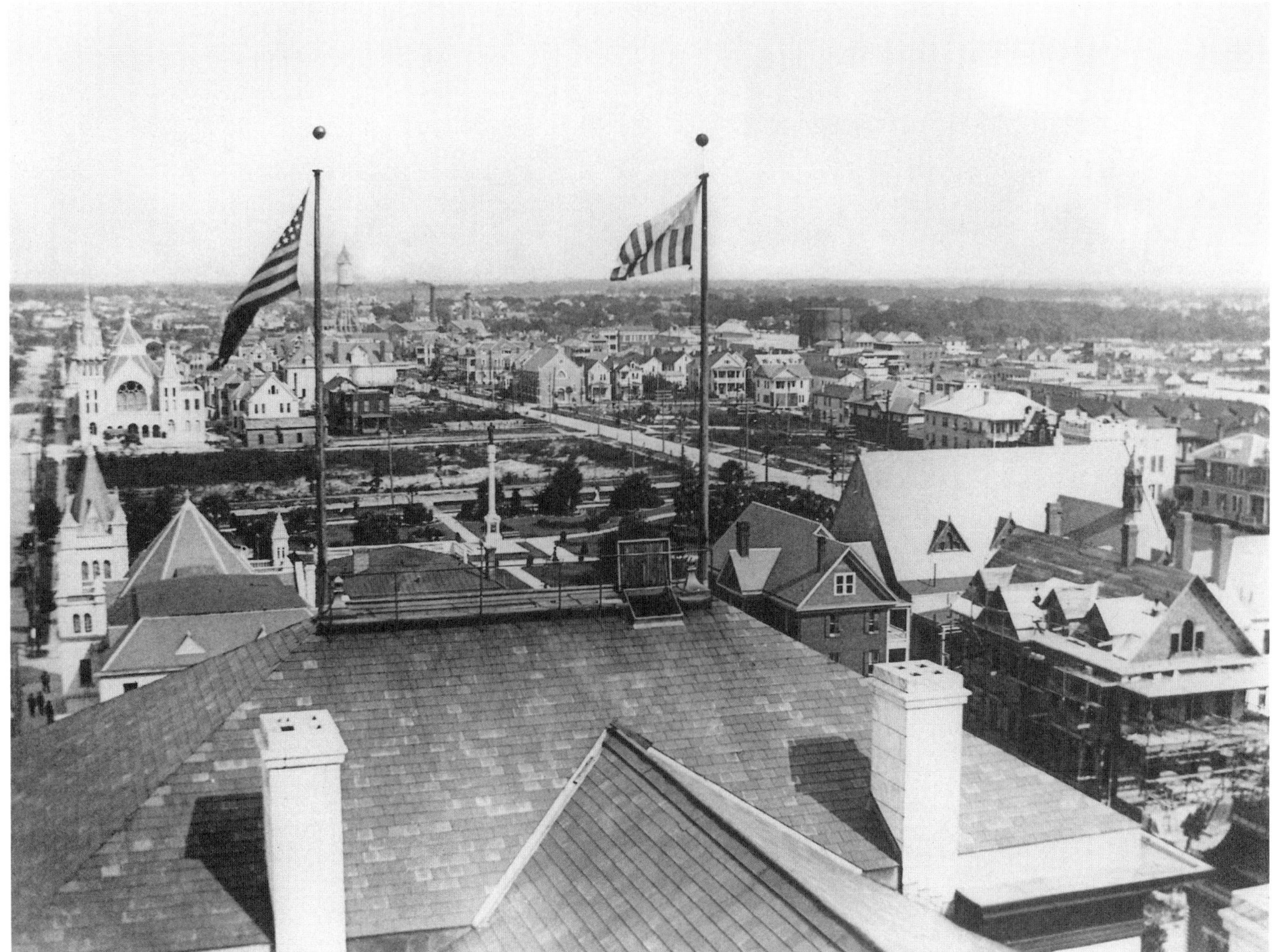

church was gone. Then I discovered, in a niche high up in the smoked wall, was the statue of the Virgin Mary.

My English grandmother had pointed her out to me one day, and I thought she was lovely. She wore beautiful snowy white and light blue robes. She was lovely, and now all the beautiful white and blue were gray and smoked and her bare feet peeped out of the ashes caught in the niche. She was discolored and blackened and her face was the dirtiest in all the world. But as I looked, I saw . . . her gentle, quiet smile of encouragement. The breeze had dusted her face, and in her smile, I found peace.

"You will help me find my mama, I know you will." So I gained hope and trudged on.

In a few days, Leah Mary Cox came along in the child's footsteps.

Her photographs of the aftermath of the fire are among the best of her pictures, and they are the most public of her pictures because she recorded an event—and, odd as it may seem to use the term, a most photogenic event—that changed the city dramatically in both its destruction and its resurrection.

Leah got her pictures.

The little girl found her mother and her way home.

The entire city was left to find its way home again after the fire. The nation pitched in. James Crooks reports in *Jacksonville After the Fire* that $225,000 in assistance was

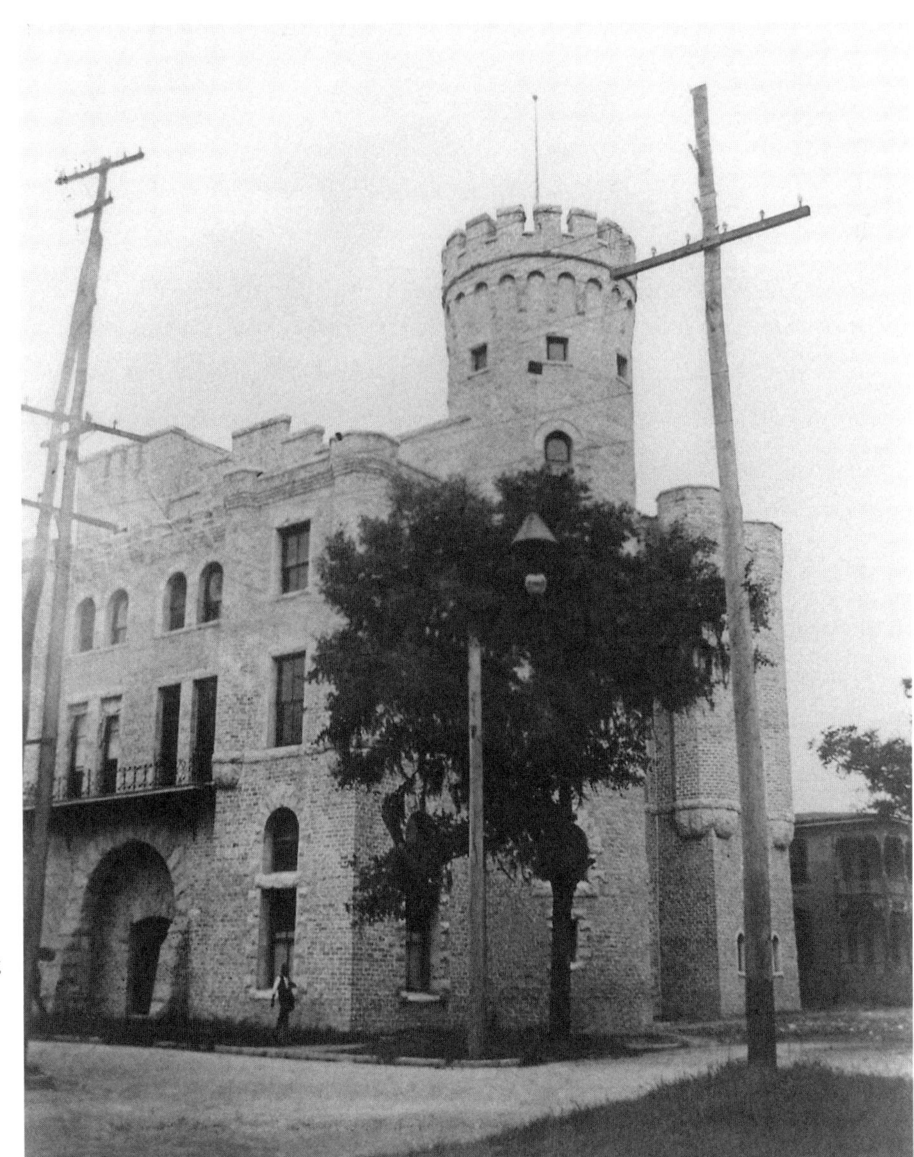

The Armory, on Market and Adams Streets, before the Great Fire, and the shell that the fire left standing.

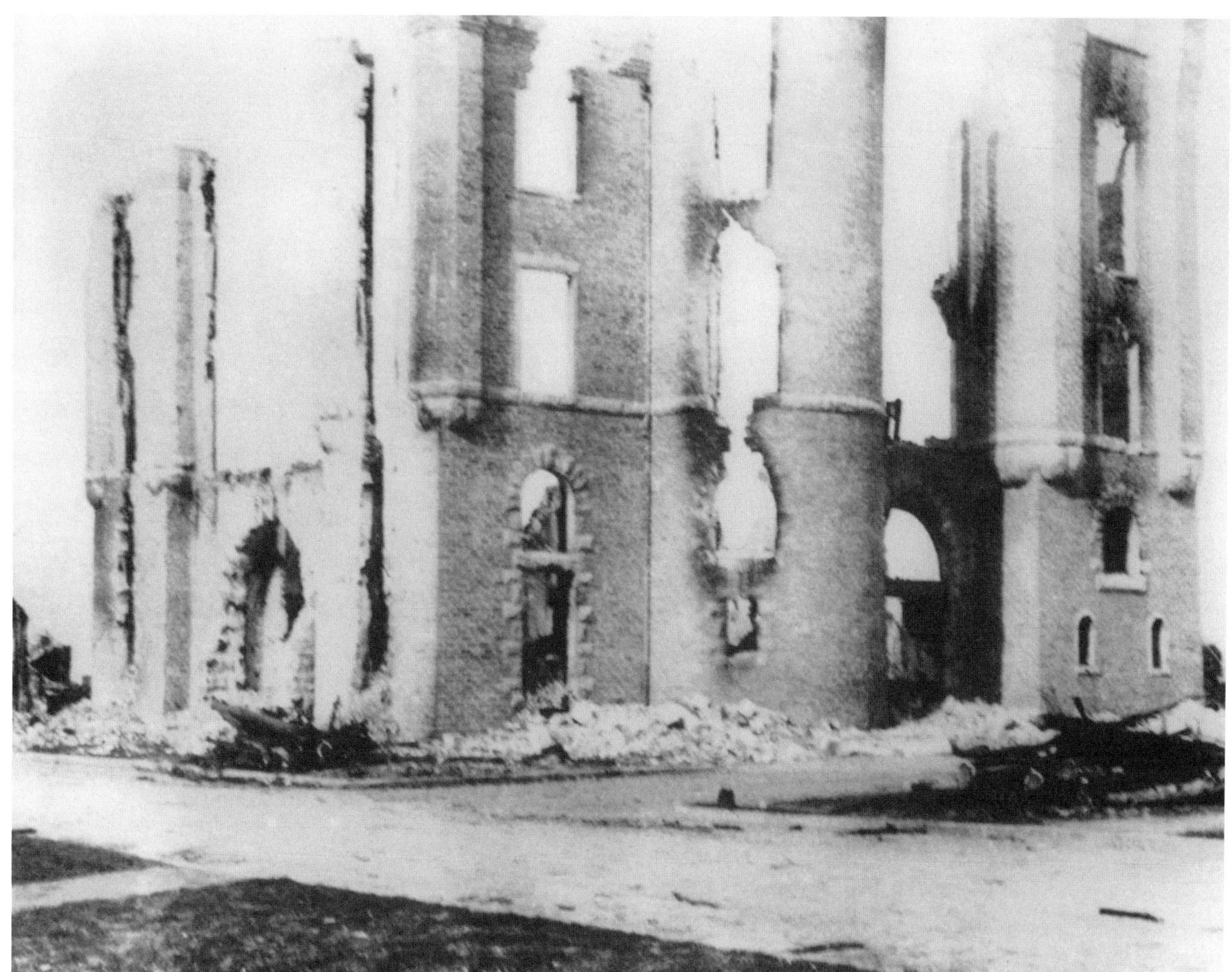

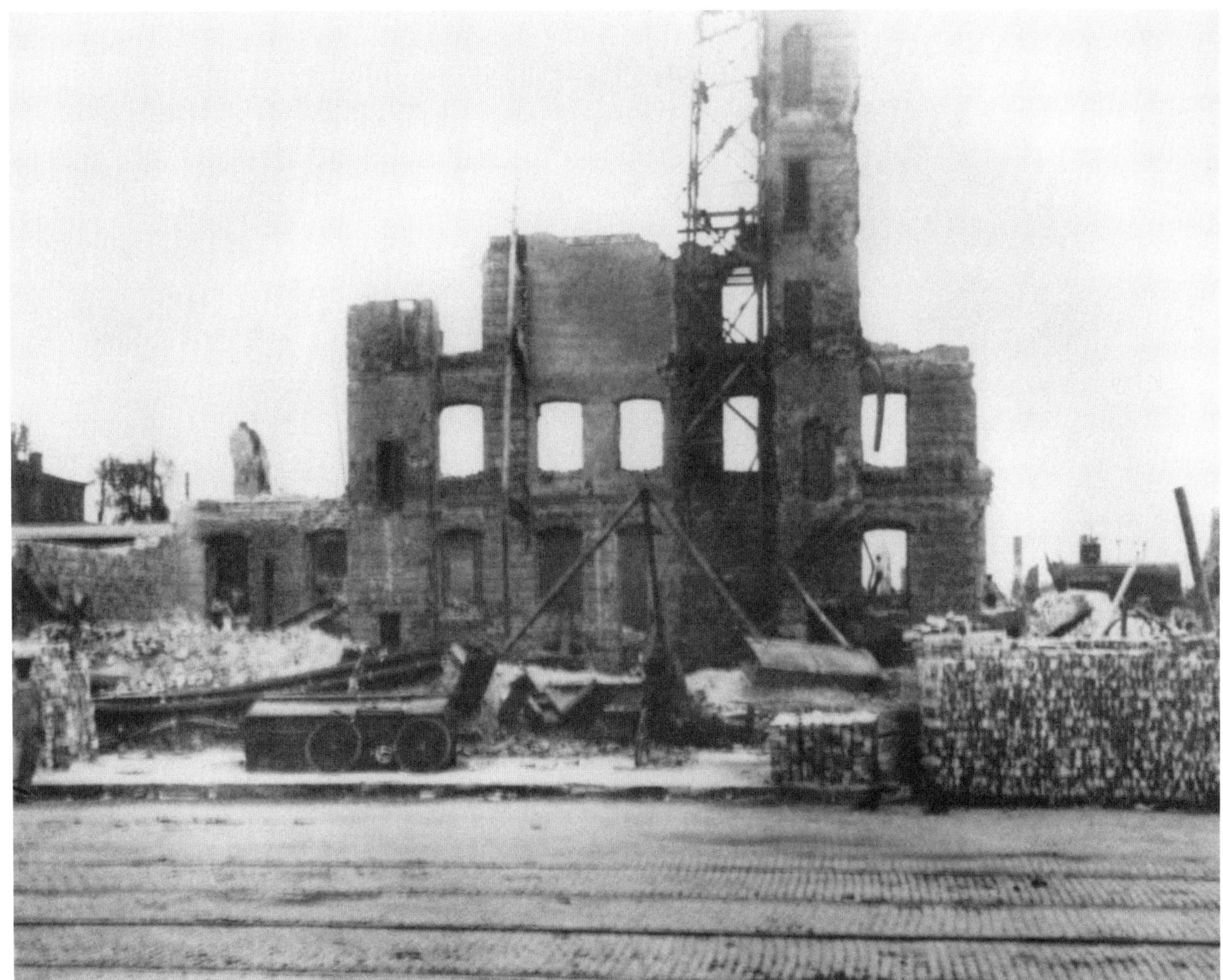

Work on the Gardner Building, on Bay Street between Laura and Main Streets, included cleaning and stacking burned bricks to reuse.

raised in cities across the country. Provisions were rushed to Jacksonville by rail and steamship. The New York State Chamber of Commerce and Merchants' Association of New York City organized a special Jacksonville Relief Commission.

A day after the fire, martial law was declared and the militia guarded the burnt-out section. Two days after the fire, food distribution stations had been set up and jobs cleaning up the debris were being filled by workers left jobless by the fire. Cots for the homeless were set up in schools. Burned-out families with financial resources were settling in rented quarters.

Tents were pitched in Hemming Park to house emergency services, including seamstresses making garments and linens for the fire's victims. There was a dispensary for medical supplies, and for information regarding sanitation and health practices during the time of emergency.

It is noticeable in Cox's photographs of the city after the fire how empty the streets are. Did she make the photographs on Sundays? There are almost no vehicles or pedestrians in the streets, no workers rebuilding the gutted buildings. Points of view from which the photographs were taken make it clear that she had to climb to the roofs of surrounding buildings for the angle she wanted. She had to make it up ladders, perhaps even climb a tree.

A young woman hauling her camera equipment through the streets, photographing

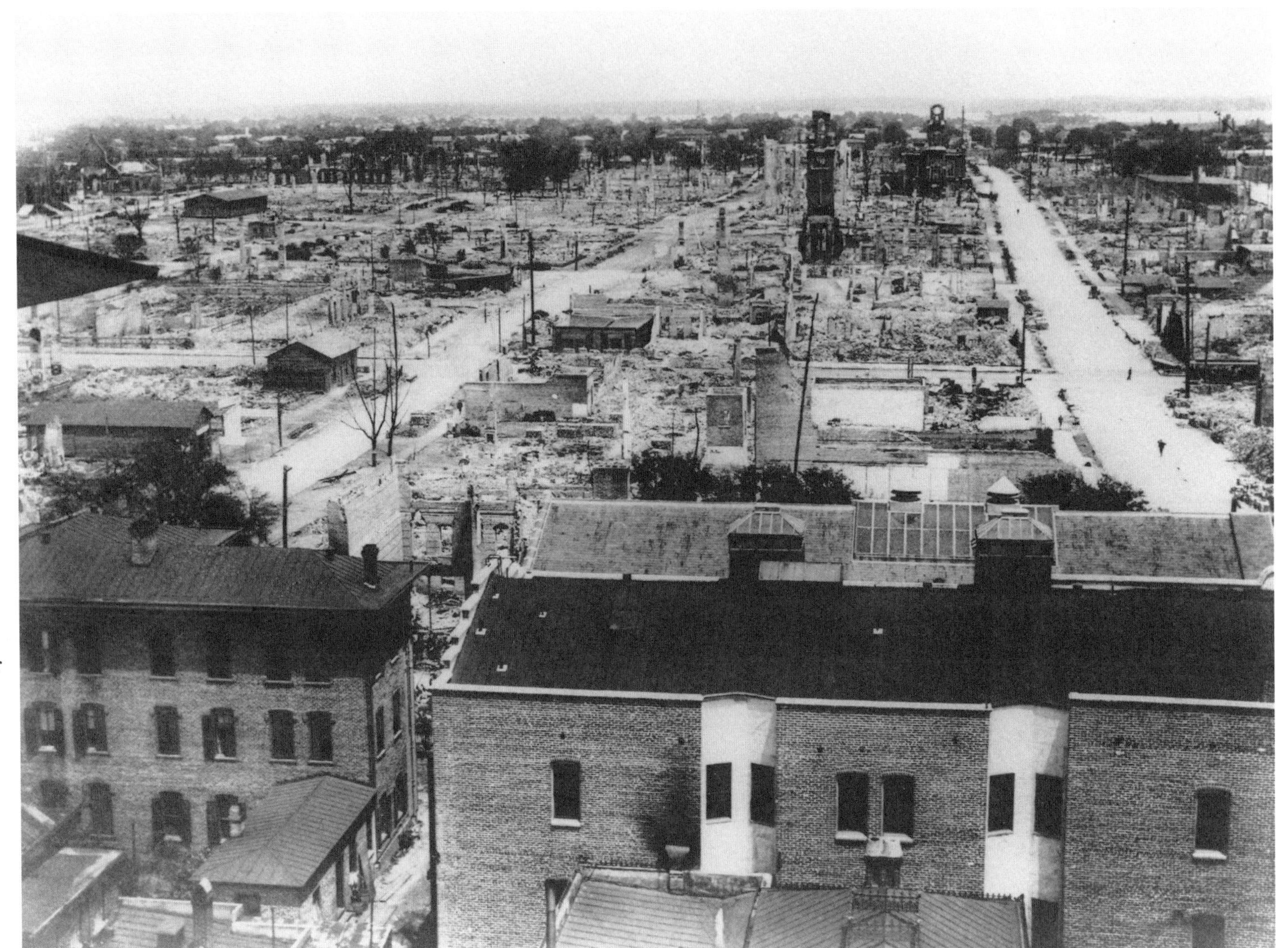

Cox prowled the ruined city with her camera days after the tragedy. Roads had been cleared, but the ashes were barely cool.

the scorched remains of the city, must have attracted some attention, though neither she nor her camera were strangers there. Nevertheless, it was a bold thing for a Victorian woman to do.

Boldness was nothing new for Cox. It was bold of her to have herded stock in Tallahassee. It was bold of her to have come, alone, to Jacksonville, bold to have brought her family to Jacksonville and found the ways to take care of them. The boldness came from necessity, whether the mission was to get a roof over her family's head, or to get the picture.

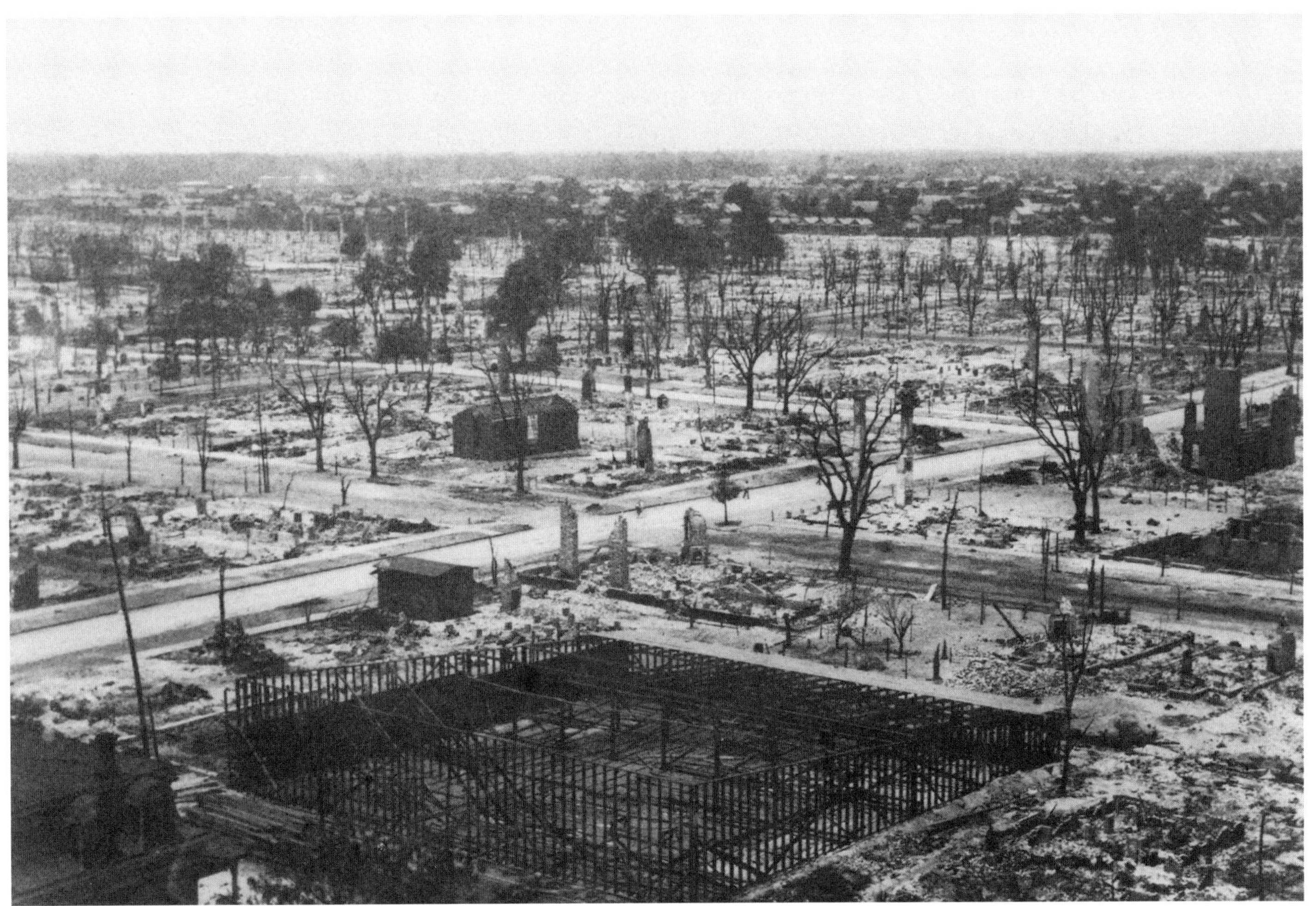

A framework rises from the blasted landscape as Jacksonville begins a comeback from its near destruction.

7

Those who knew her remember Leah Cox, in her old age, as daunting and austere. But her photographs show that, as a young woman, she was intrigued with the bright side of Jacksonville, with its entertainment centers and entertainers. The photographs show that she liked to ramble to nearby environs for picnics and sailing parties.

Jacksonville was the entertainment capital of the South in the early years of the twentieth century, and Cox was no stay-at-home.

Besides stage shows, vaudeville, concerts, even opera, there were movies and amusement parks.

The city's first amusement park was the Ostrich Farm. It opened in 1898 and offered an almost unimaginable variety of things to do with ostriches, in addition to looking at them. The visitor could ride in a cart pulled by an ostrich, watch ostriches race, even saddle up an ostrich and take a ride.

The ostriches spent summers in Atlantic City, and their annual return to Jacksonville was an event that attracted citizens, visitors, and, of course, the press.

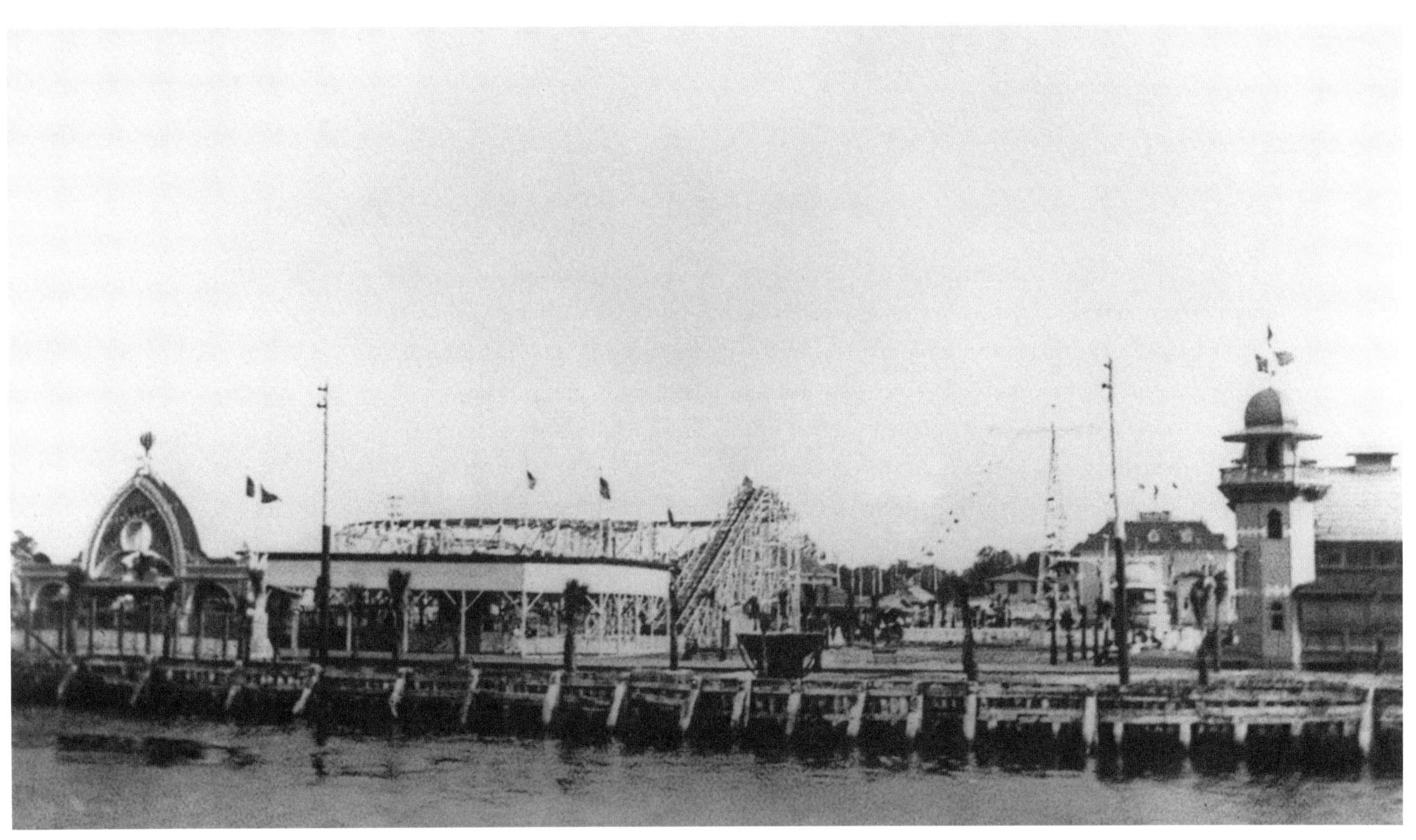

Dixieland Park, 1908, "the Coney Island of the South," just a ferryboat ride away across the St. Johns River from Jacksonville, was among Cox's favorite subjects.

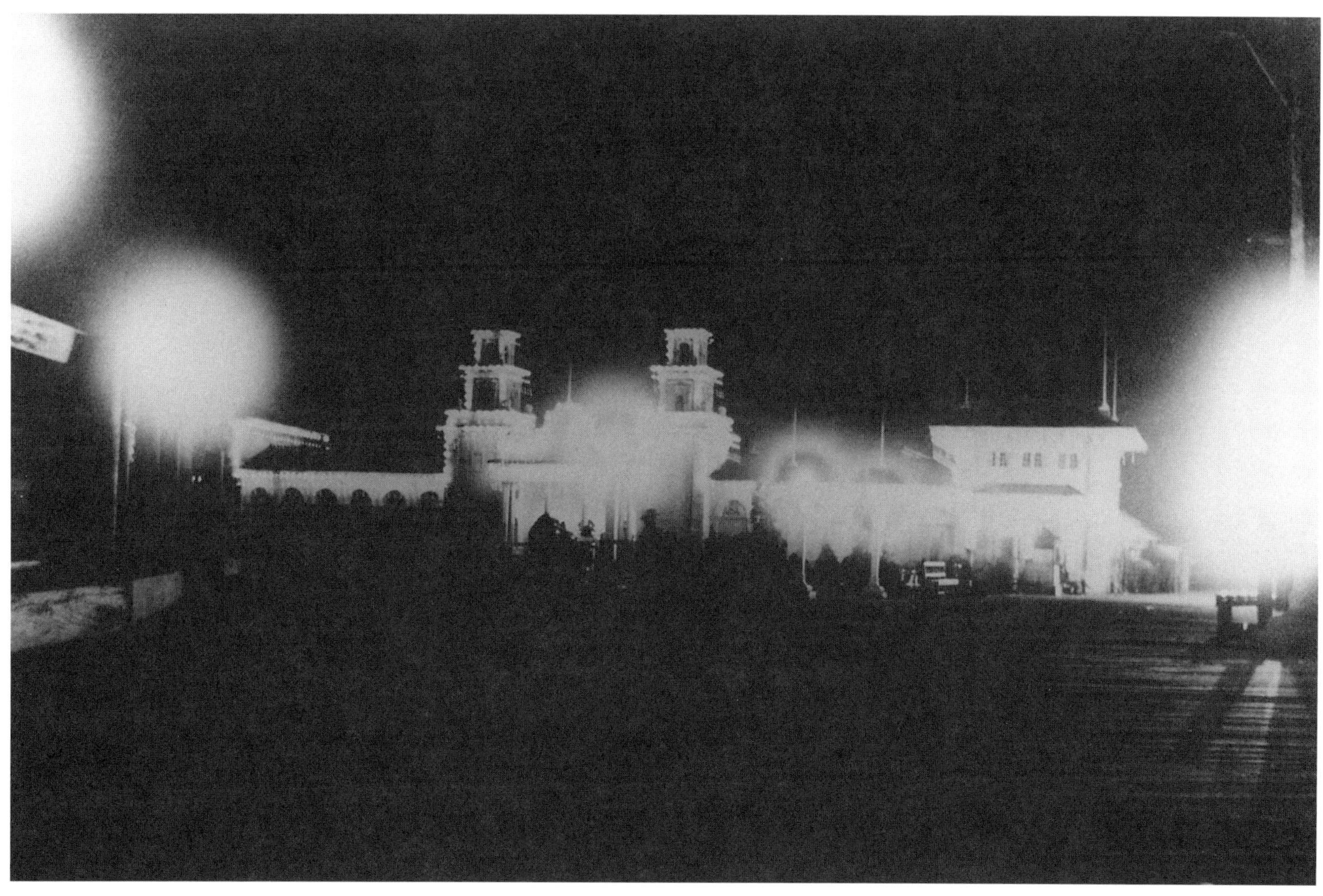

At night, thousands of electric lights and their reflections in the St. Johns turned Dixieland Park into a magical land. This study is one of the rare examples of night photography in Leah Cox's work. Usually, she worked with outside available daylight.

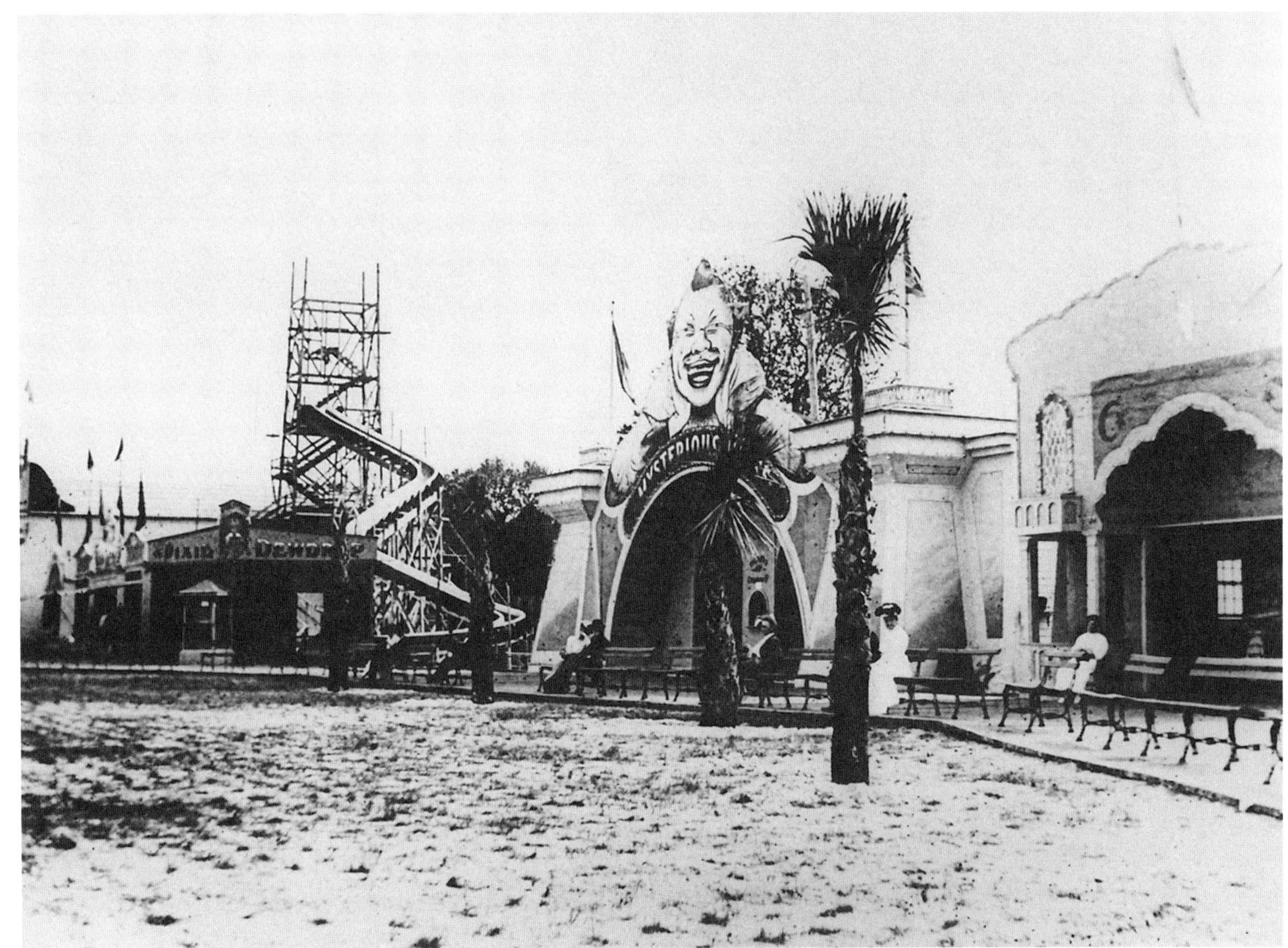

Attractions at Dixieland Park included a 160-foot slide called the Dixie Dewdrop and the Mysterious House funhouse.

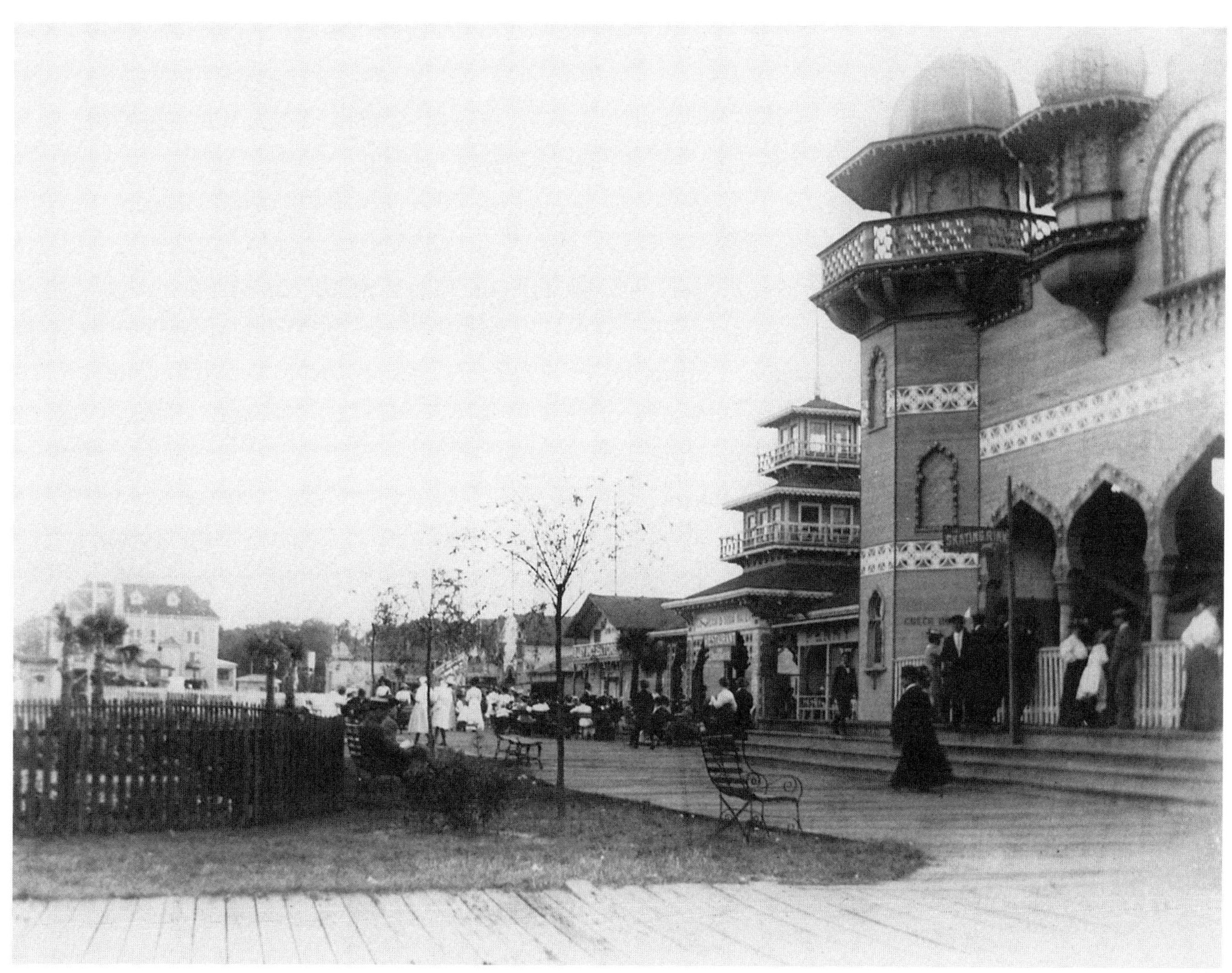

Shops, restaurants, attractions, and a skating rink with a Moorish design lined Dixieland Park's broad boardwalk.

Over the years, the Ostrich Farm expanded its attractions to include a menagerie that featured Florida alligators, as well as exotic jungle animals.

There were balloon ascents, parachute jumps, a roller coaster. There were dancing, swimming, refreshments.

The Jacksonville Street Railways operated Phoenix Park, another amusement park, to encourage passengers to use the railway on Sunday. In time, the Ostrich Farm relocated to Phoenix Park, much expanding its attractions. The ostriches kept on racing, however, pulling sulkies or ridden by jockeys.

Most famous of the racing birds was Cyclone.

A grandstand built at Phoenix Park in 1907 provided a place for the management to stage the Holmes Wild West Show. There were high-wire acts, Spanish dancers, lion tamers, and magicians. Sharpshooter Annie Oakley put on an exhibition at Phoenix Park, and Carrie Nation showed up there to warn against the evils of alcohol.

Actress Mabel Paige appeared for several seasons at Phoenix Park. She was Jacksonville's most famous actress, and she was a friend—and client—of Leah Cox. There are several pictures, candid and portraits, of Mabel Paige in Cox's collection. There are no "Made by Leah" tags hanging from the actress's stunning hats, but it is natural to conclude that Cox made the hats as well as the pictures.

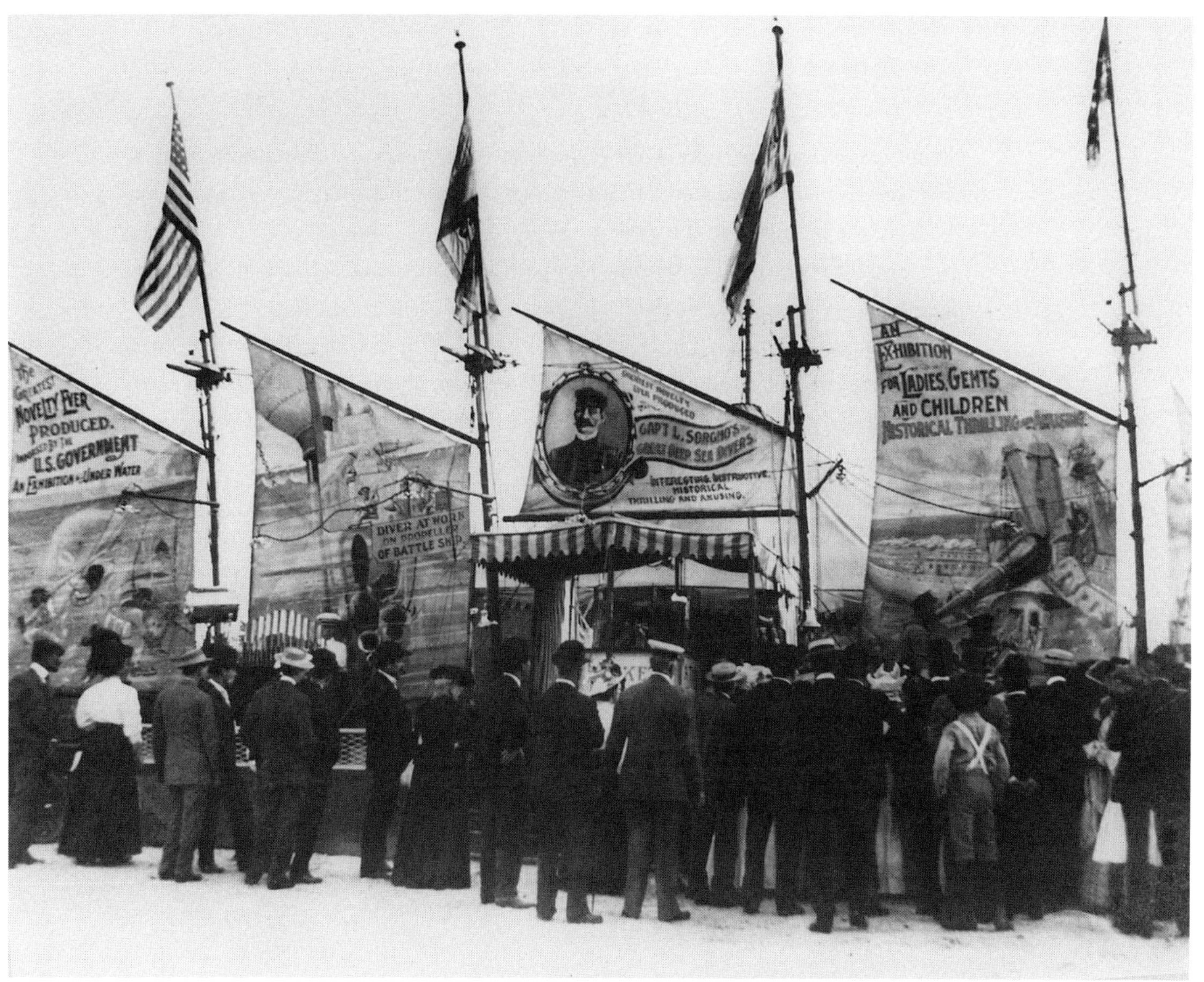

One of Dixieland Park's most popular and novel diversions, an exhibition by Capt. L. Sorgho's Great Deep Sea Divers, was touted as fit for "ladies, gents, and children." Deemed "historical, thrilling, and amusing," the attraction, "endorsed by the U.S. government," showed divers at work repairing a battleship's propeller.

Paige was a star of the Jacksonville scene in the early years of the twentieth century. Indeed, she was acknowledged by those who saw her as "the finest actress ever to appear before the footlights in this city."

She was, for seventy of her seventy-four years, a professional actress, and she spent many of those years in Jacksonville.

"Miss Paige first appeared in Jacksonville in 1906," *Times-Union* staff writer James C. Craig wrote in Paige's obituary in 1954. "The small, plump brunette was the heroine in hundreds of dramas here and played her way right into the hearts of many theatergoers. She was Jacksonville's sweetheart for a number of years."

Her run at the Phoenix Park Casino lasted four summers.

She also played at the Dixie Theatre at Dixieland Park, Jacksonville's famous "Coney Island of the South" across the river from Phoenix Park.

Paige also worked with her own stock company, which was managed by her husband, Charles Ritchie. From the amusement parks, they moved the show downtown to the Orpheum Theatre, which was renamed the Paige Theatre for her season.

She was remarkably successful and once broke all Jacksonville box office records when she played to more than twelve thousand people in six performances of *Forty-Five Minutes from Broadway.*

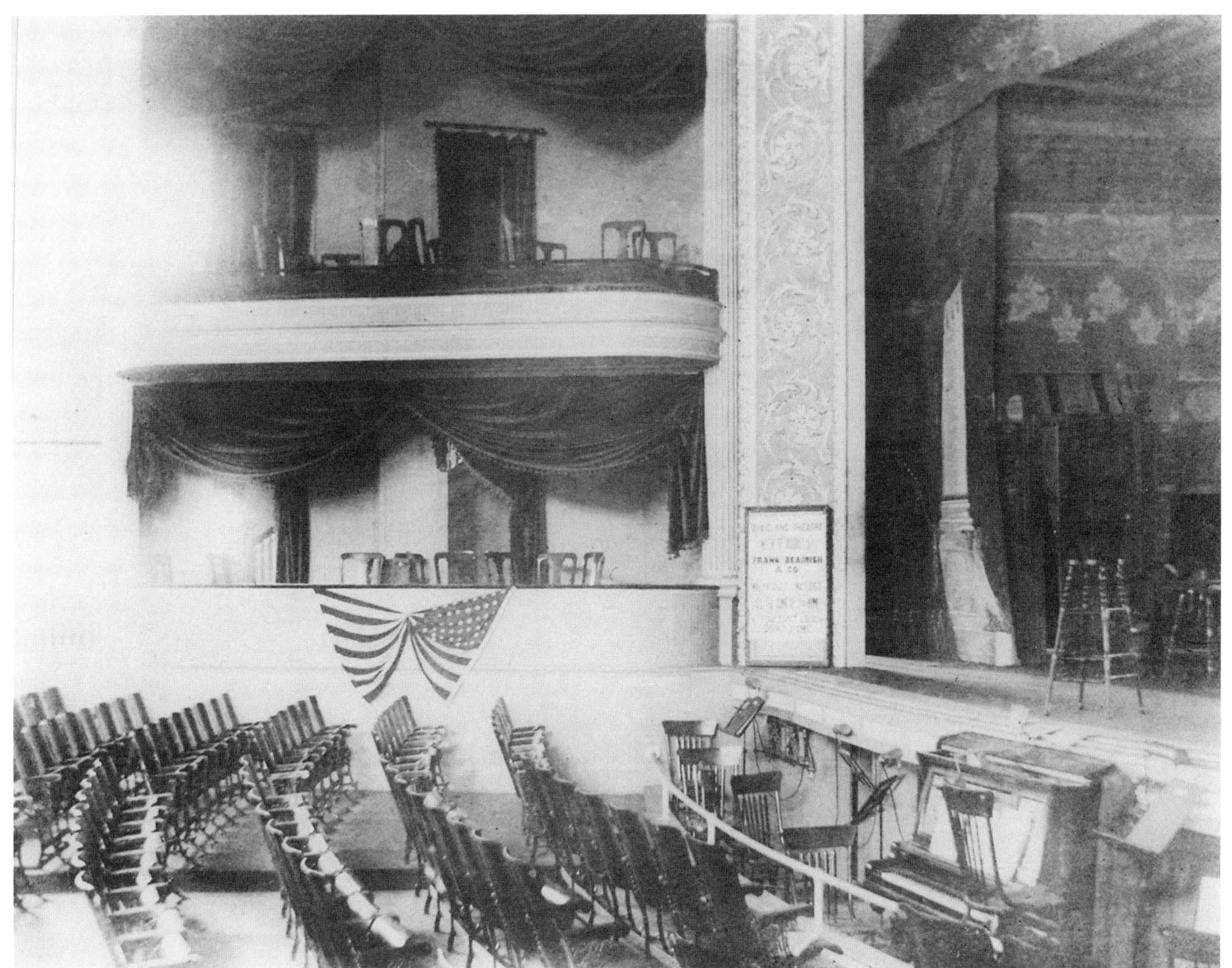

The Dixie Theatre at Dixieland Park offered plays, musical reviews, and lectures in indoor comfort. "Jacksonville's sweetheart," Mabel Paige, regularly played the Dixie.

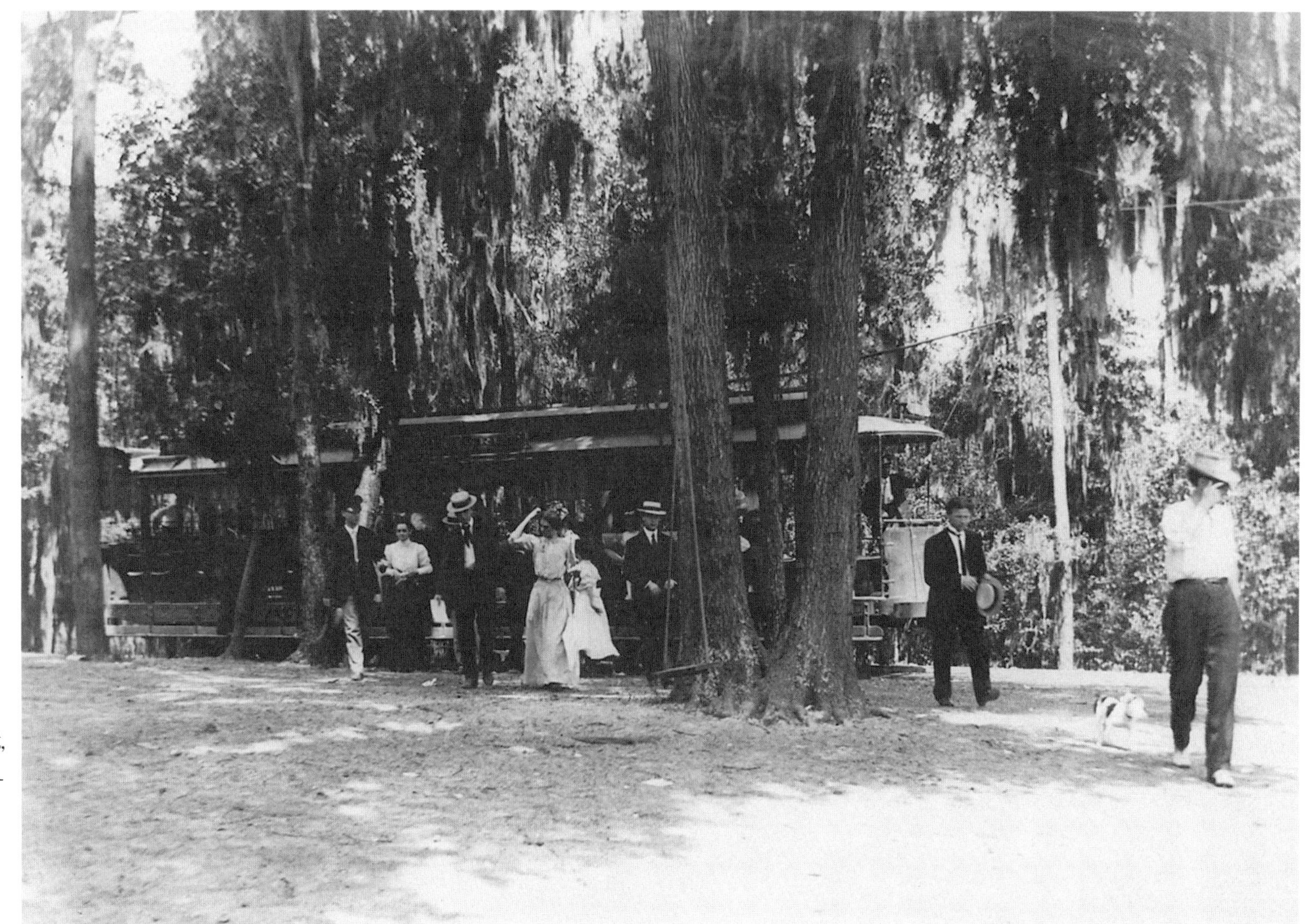

A candid photo of actress Mabel Paige, holding onto her hat, with her husband, Charles Ritchie, on her right, arriving for a performance at Phoenix Park.

Paige followed the movie business to Hollywood and had a long career playing featured, though not starring, roles in scores of movies. There is no way to know, but it is understandable to wonder if Leah Cox, as an old woman, went to see her old friend in the movies. The women died within a year of one another.

Cox made many photographs of all of Jacksonville's entertainment sites, including Dixieland Park and the beaches, a favorite outing when rail branches linked the city to the beach in 1900 and when a narrow brick road to the shore was finally opened in 1910.

Dixieland Park was Jacksonville's most amazing attraction.

It opened in 1907 on the south side of the river, directly across from downtown, a ferryboat ride away. It had everything for the amusement of the public. It was fabulous. There was a roller coaster, a 160-foot slide called the Dixie Dewdrop, a giant merry-go-round, a Japanese tea garden, a spooky attraction called Mysterious House Doomsday, burro rides, shops, dancing, thousands of electric lights, a children's playground, ragtime, acrobats, theater, music, even a photographic gallery. Fires in 1909 and 1910 set back the park, and eventually it closed, the end of an era.

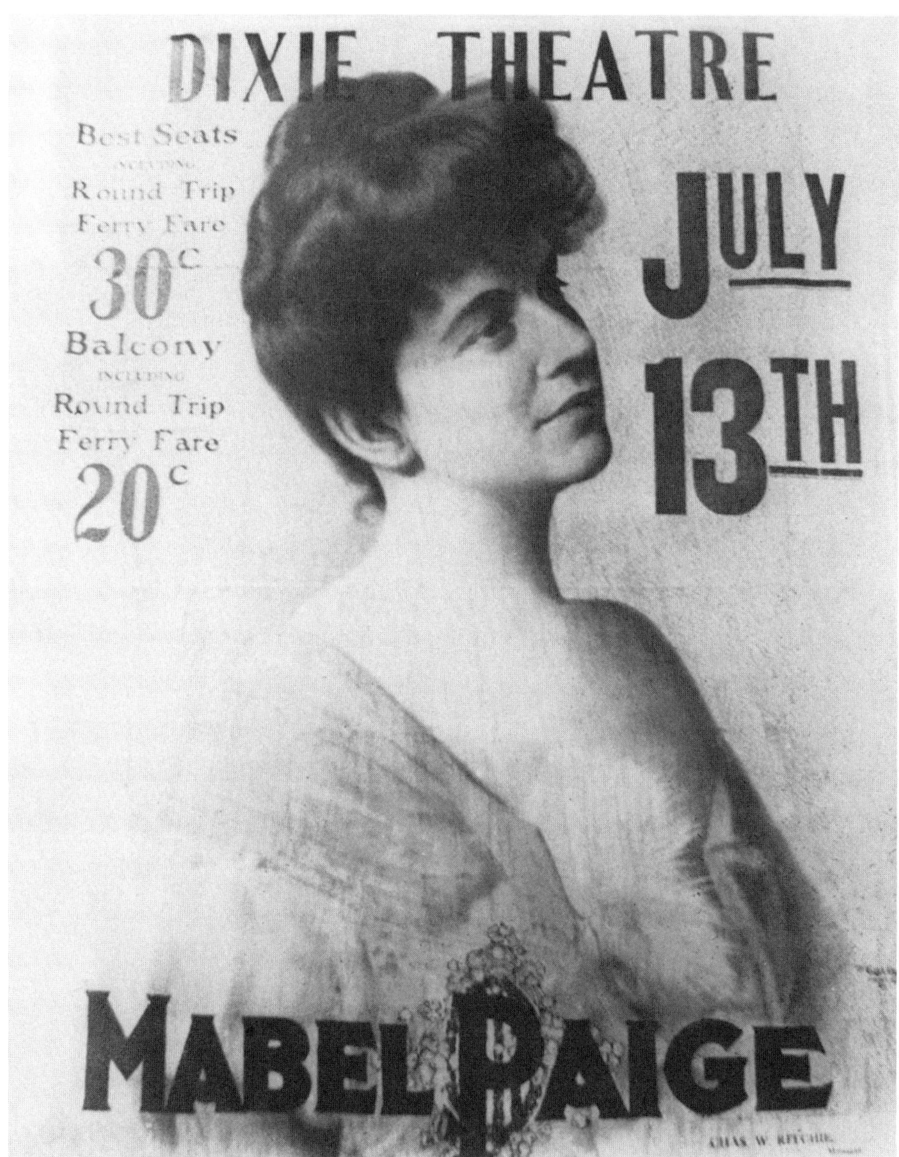

The best seats in the house for this Mabel Paige performance at the Dixie Theatre cost 30 cents and included round-trip ferry fare from Jacksonville to Dixieland Park.

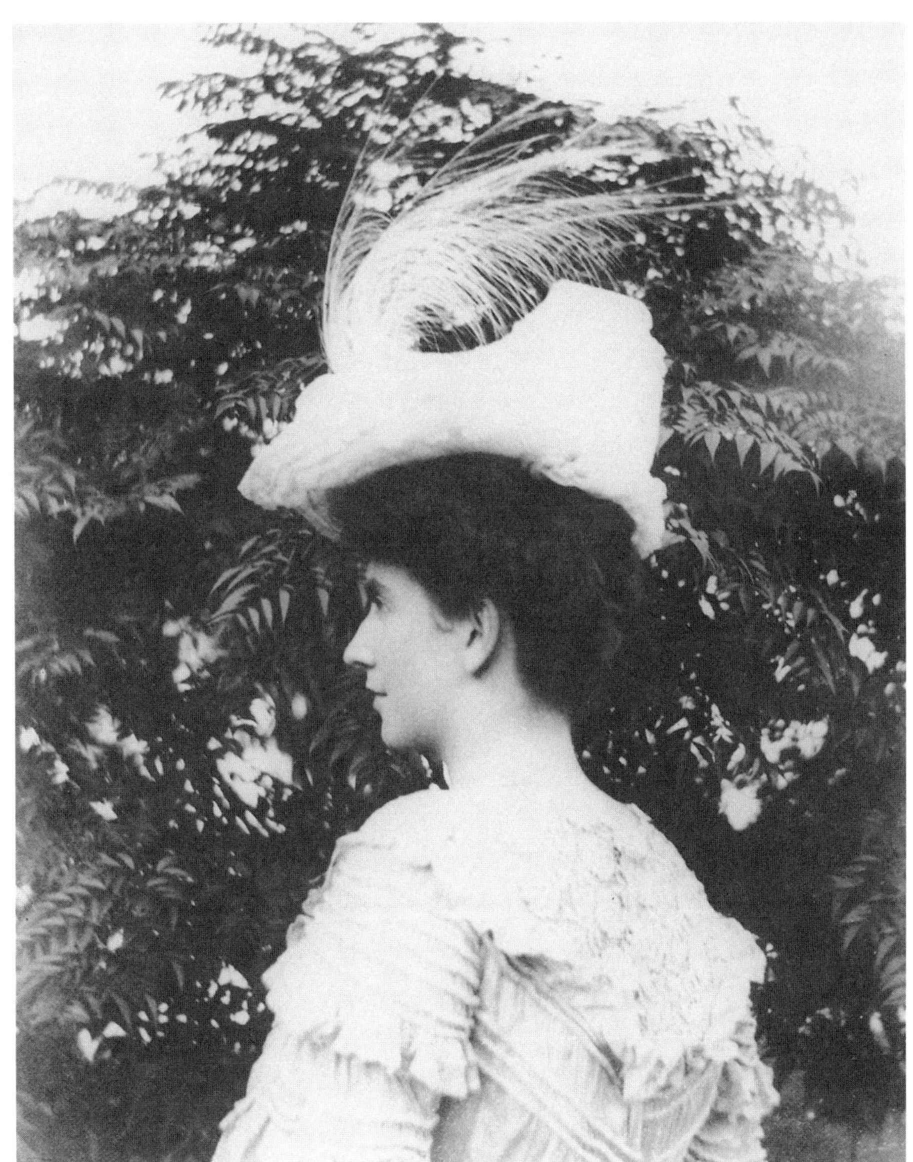

Mabel Paige poses in a hat designed by Cox.

A Tin Lizzie approaches a downtown Jacksonville corner that houses the Orpheum Cigar Store and the Mabel Paige Theatre, where the popular actress played in *The Avengers.* Before Paige left Jacksonville and built a successful movie career as a featured player in Hollywood, she starred in shows in the city, at Phoenix Park, and at Dixieland Park.

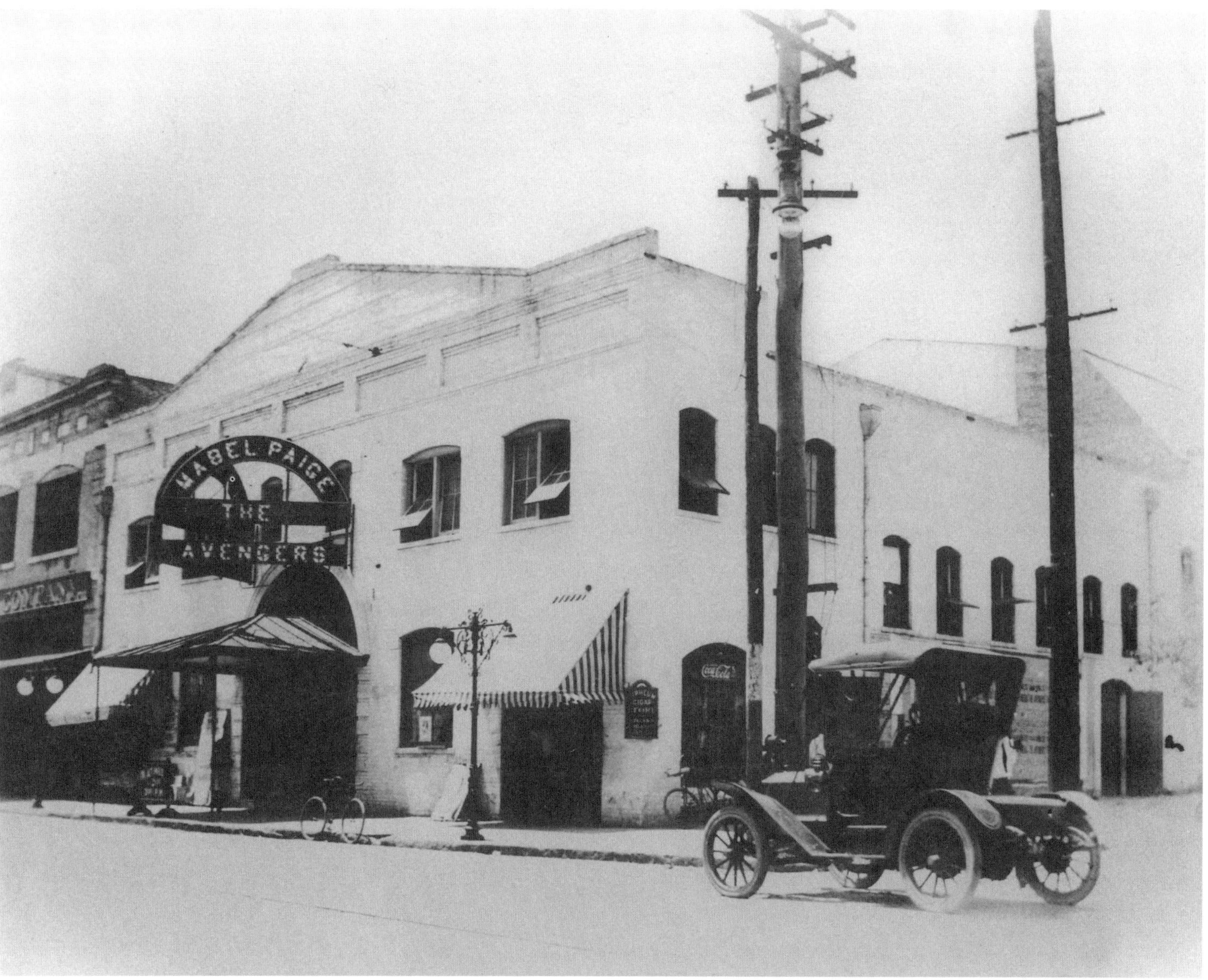

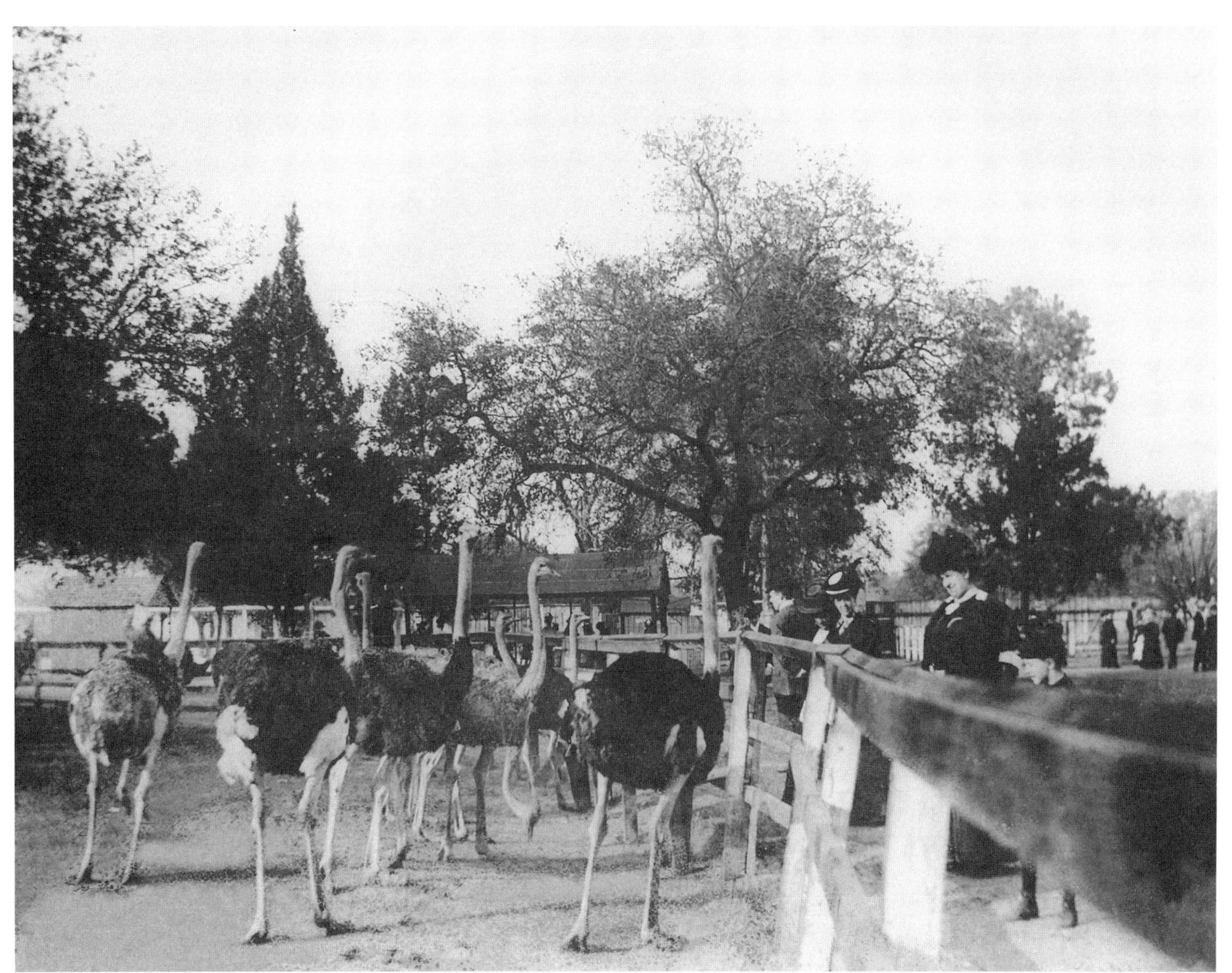

The Ostrich Farm, Jacksonville's first amusement park, opened in 1898 and offered visitors the opportunity to ride in a cart pulled by an ostrich, watch the big birds race, and even ride one of them. The ostriches spent summers in Atlantic City.

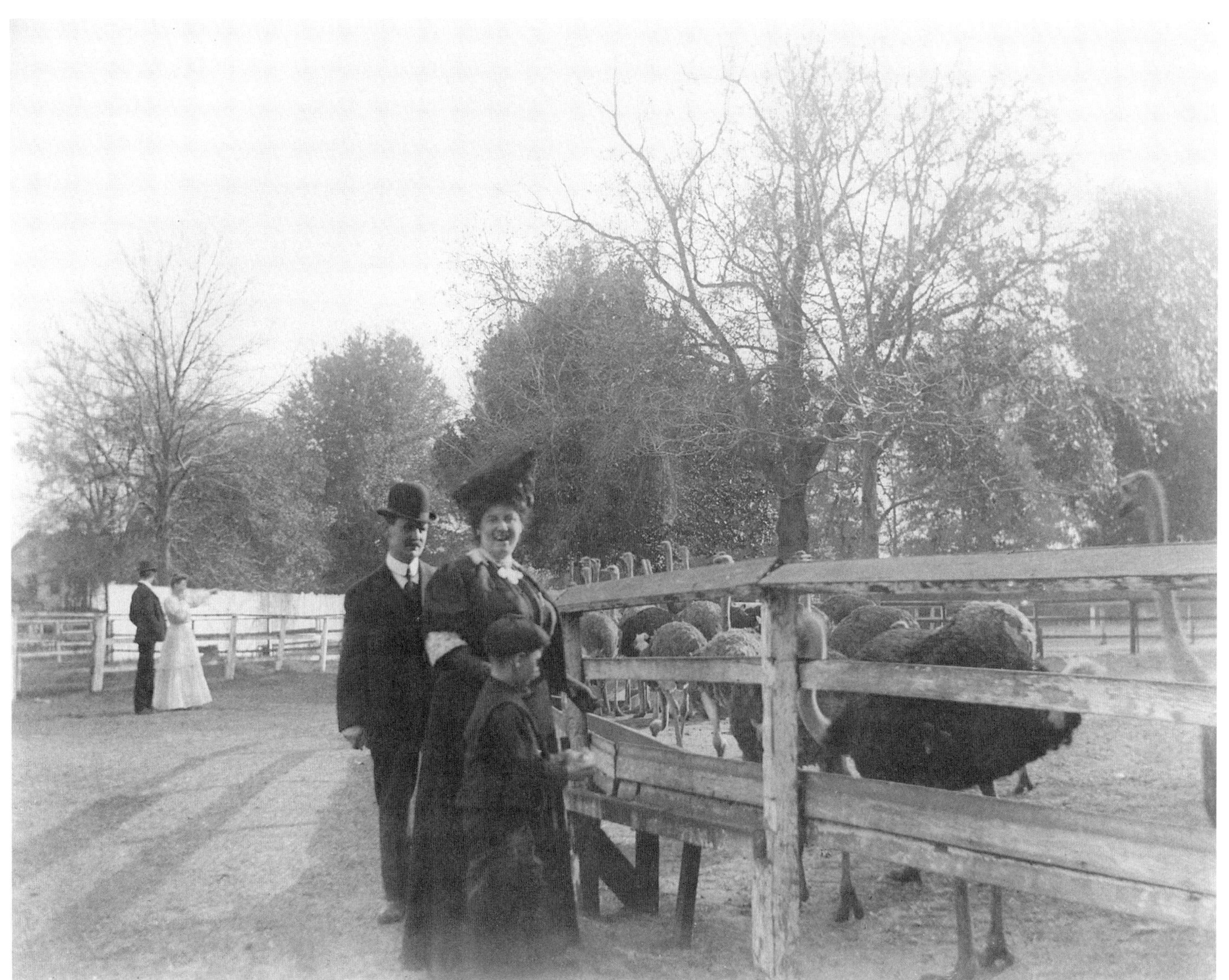

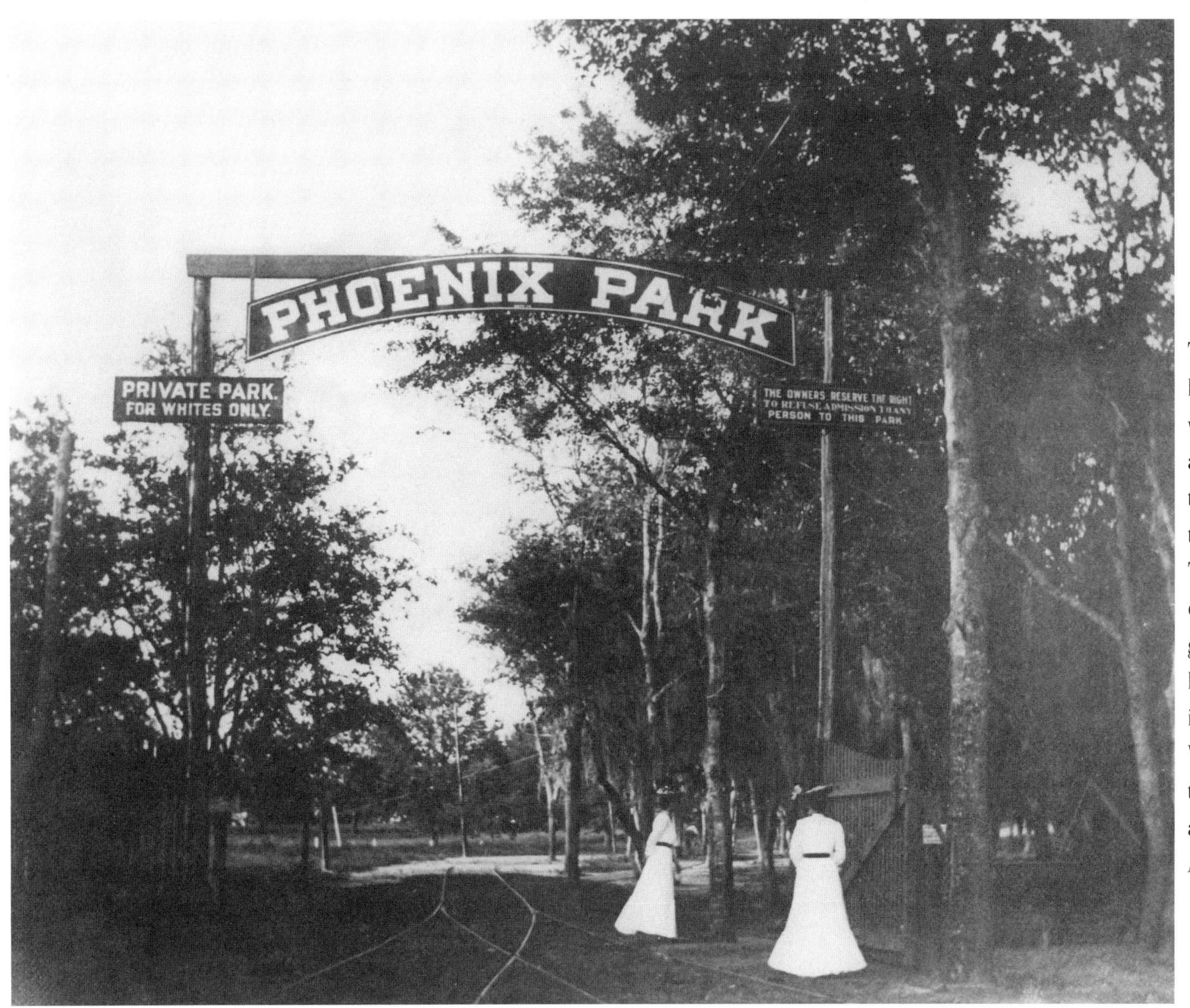

The Jacksonville Street Railways opened the whites-only Phoenix Park at the turn of the century to encourage passengers to ride the rail on Sunday. The Ostrich Farm relocated to Phoenix, and a grandstand built in 1907 hosted outdoor shows, including the Holmes Wild West Show, lion tamers, high-wire artists, and famed sharpshooter Annie Oakley.

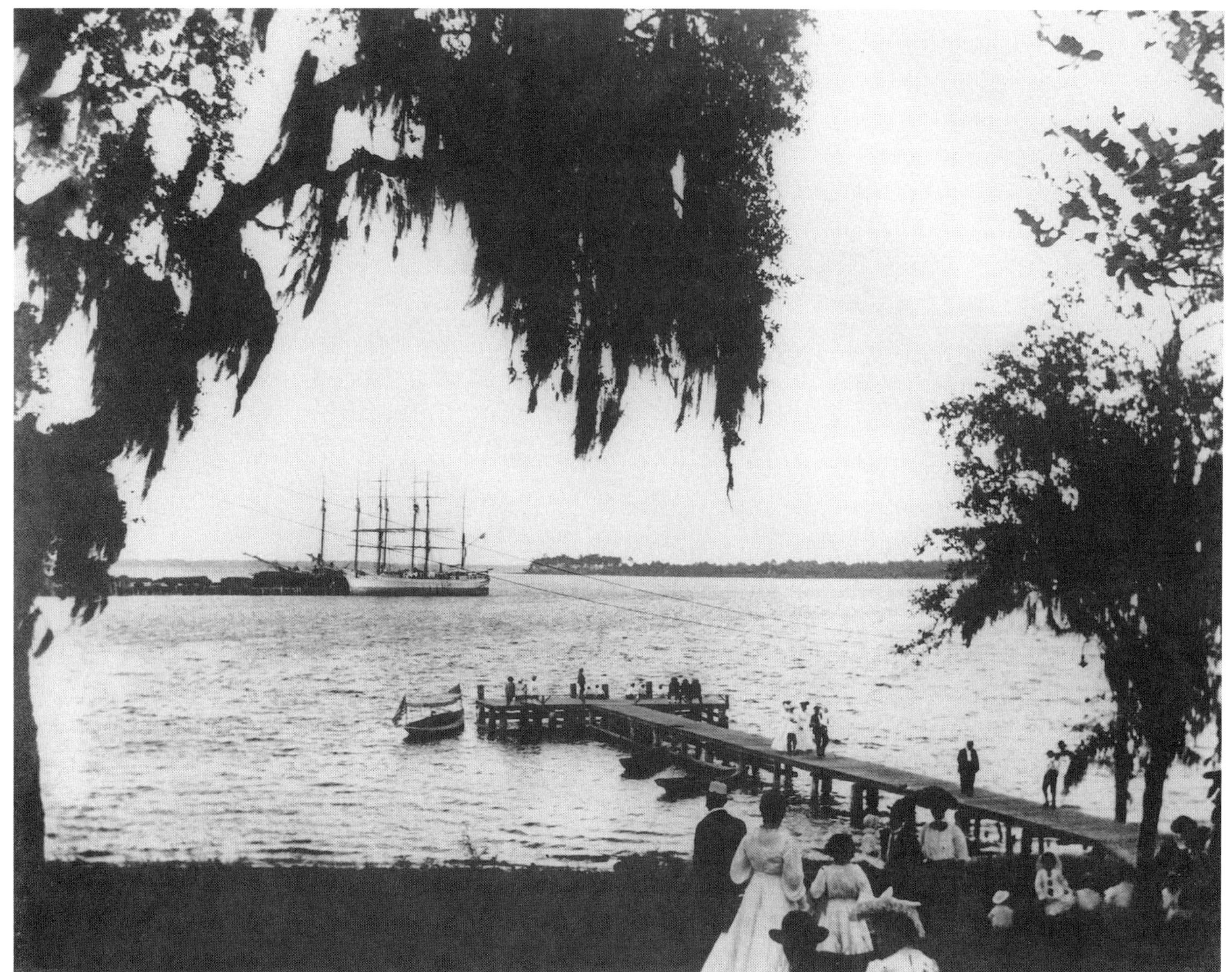

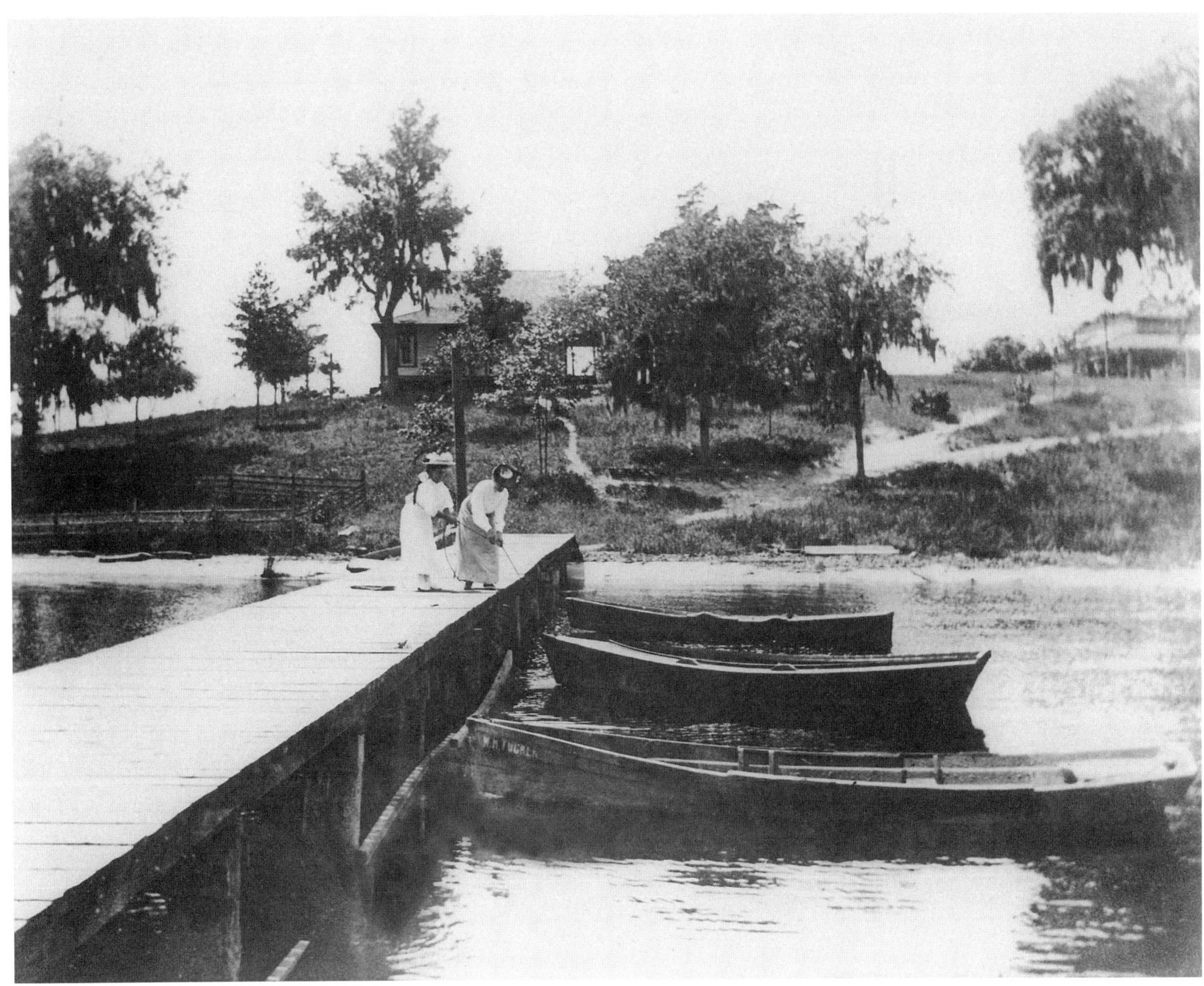

Visitors could reach Phoenix Park by the St. Johns River as well as by rail.

8

When Leah Cox's mother, Ellen, and her sister Esther, long an invalid because of her bad heart, died within six weeks of one another in the autumn of 1890, Leah Cox bought a large burial plot in Jacksonville's Evergreen Cemetery. A few days after Esther's burial, Leah had the bodies of their father, William Henry Cox, and of their brother William John Cox, who had died at fourteen in Tallahassee, moved to Evergreen. She was ever a gatherer. And she wanted everyone together in death, as she had gathered the family together in life.

By 1919, the Cox household was down to Leah and her sister Lenah. Leah and Lenah bought property on Jacksonville's west side after World War I, uncleared land on Fishweir Creek. On weekends and long summer afternoons, the sisters and their brother Rowland rode streetcars to the property, where they chopped brush and grubbed out palmettos.

They bought a surplus barracks tent and set it up on the property.

Then they had a wood floor put down and sides and a roof framed, and they dropped the tent over the wood framework.

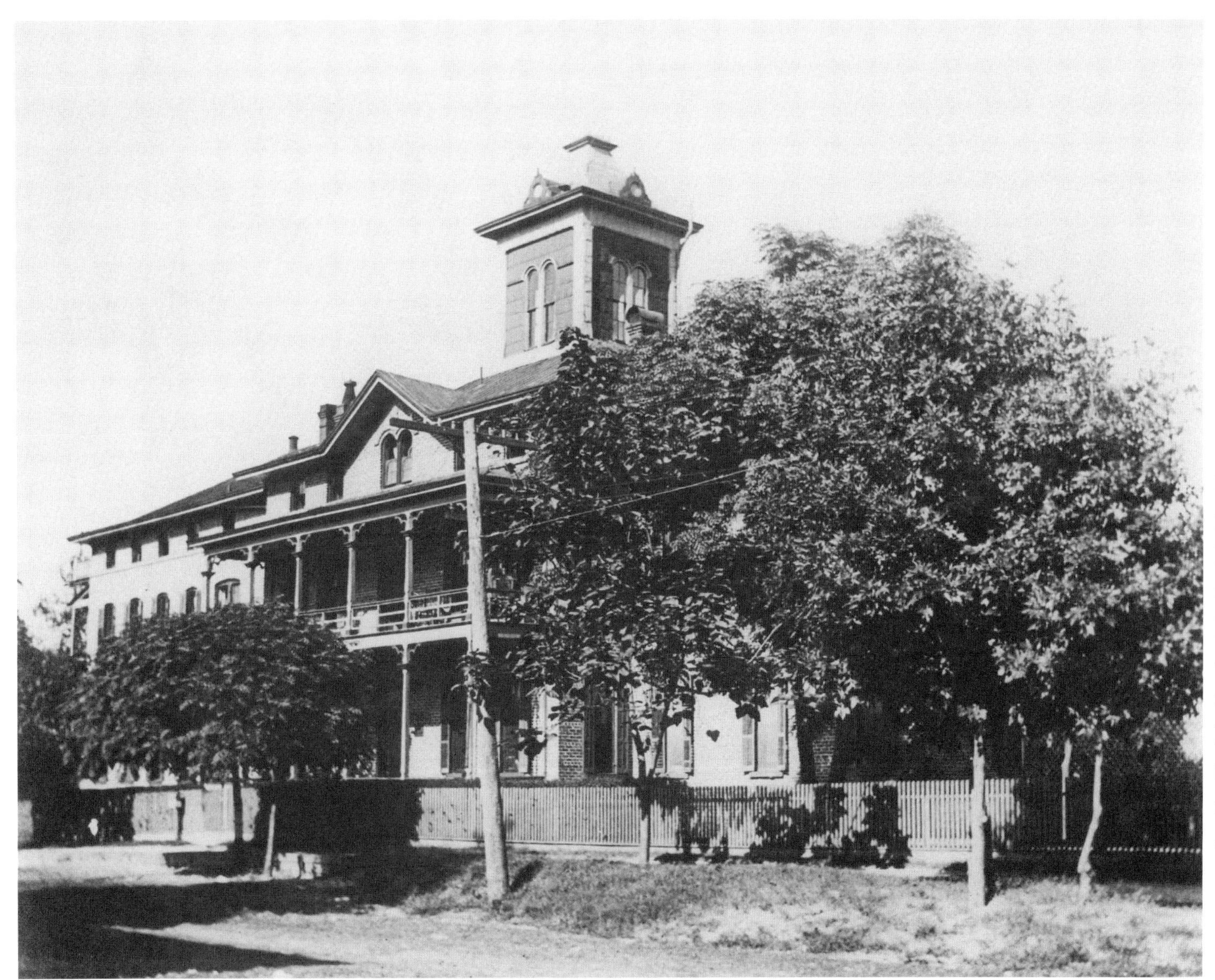

Leah Cox documented Jacksonville landmarks after the fire, including St. Luke's Hospital. Built during the yellow fever epidemic, the building survived the fire and continued as a medical center until 1914.

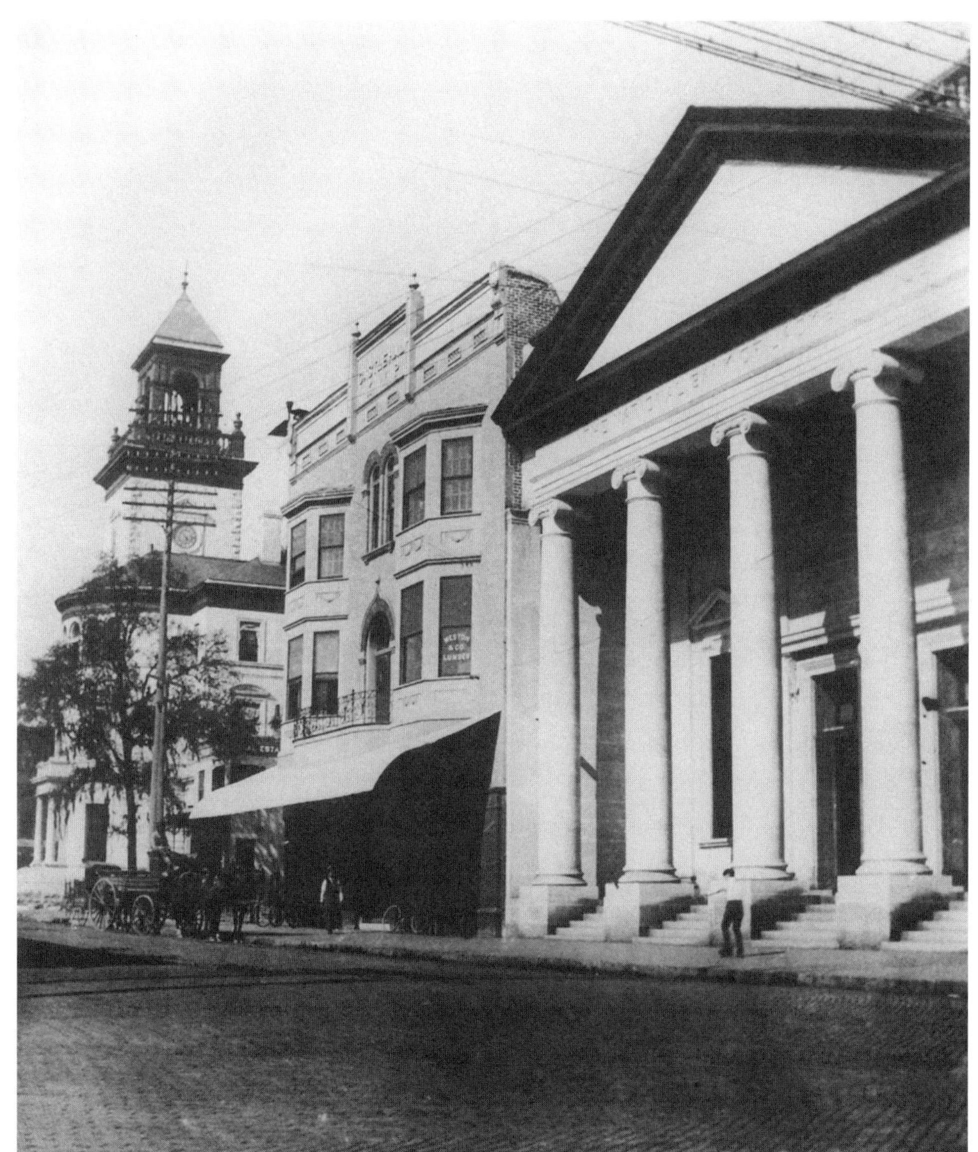

The National Bank of Jacksonville was one of several banks that lined Forsyth Street. Others included Barnett Bank and Atlantic Bank, creating the city's financial center.

It was an interesting beginning, but Leah Cox was not satisfied. She drew plans for an expansion and haunted lumber yards and salvage yards, buying seconds and used lumber. In 1926, the family doubled the size of the house by adding a second story, and that is where Leah Cox lived the rest of her life. She worked as a seamstress and milliner and often as a companion to Dr. Jay Durkee's wife during her pregnancies.

She set up a darkroom to process her photographs.

Lenah Cox never married, and she went to work "part time" for a drug company and retired fifty years later.

Leah's sister Ellen married Harry Hubert Scott, the son of a pioneer family that operated a mill in Mandarin, hence the present-day Scott Mill Road.

Her brother Frank lost his arm in an unexplained gunshot accident during the Spanish-American War and was unable to work thereafter.

Rowland became a plumber and moved to Miami.

No one remembers when it happened, or where, or why. But Leah Cox's old box camera was ruined in the rain.

Cox bought another camera, but she was never again satisfied with her pictures.

She packed up her boxes of glass negatives and stored them in the basement of the house she built out of the surplus tent and second-hand lumber. Her vision of the Great Fire, of Dixieland Park, of steamboats and sailboats on the St. Johns River, of

Pablo Beach and St. Andrew's parish, of Mabel Paige and two generations of Cox children, was saved like time in a bottle. One of Cox's nieces has wondered if she thought, at some time, of going into business as a professional photographer. The stock of negatives she kept so carefully may suggest that it crossed Cox's mind. But there is no way to know.

It was not unusual for women to pursue photography as a hobby or a profession a hundred years ago. Many were portraitists, and a few were becoming photojournalists.

In 1899, Richard Hines Jr. told the Art League of Mobile, Alabama: "There is no more suitable work for a woman than photography, whether she takes it up with a view of making it a profession, or simply as a delightful pastime to give pleasure to herself and others! She is by nature peculiarly fitted for the work, and photography is becoming more and more recognized as a field of endeavor peculiarly suited to women."

It is notable that half the participants in the exhibition of New American Photography taken to London in 1900 were women.

Cox was not out of time if she had set out to become a professional photographer.

But her responsibilities did not favor her pursuit of other than a conventional life. She was the head of her family, thus an anchor. The role shaped her life and her behavior. The house she built for her family has been home to a succession of Coxes for the past eighty years. Somewhere inside the architectural patchwork of the sturdy little

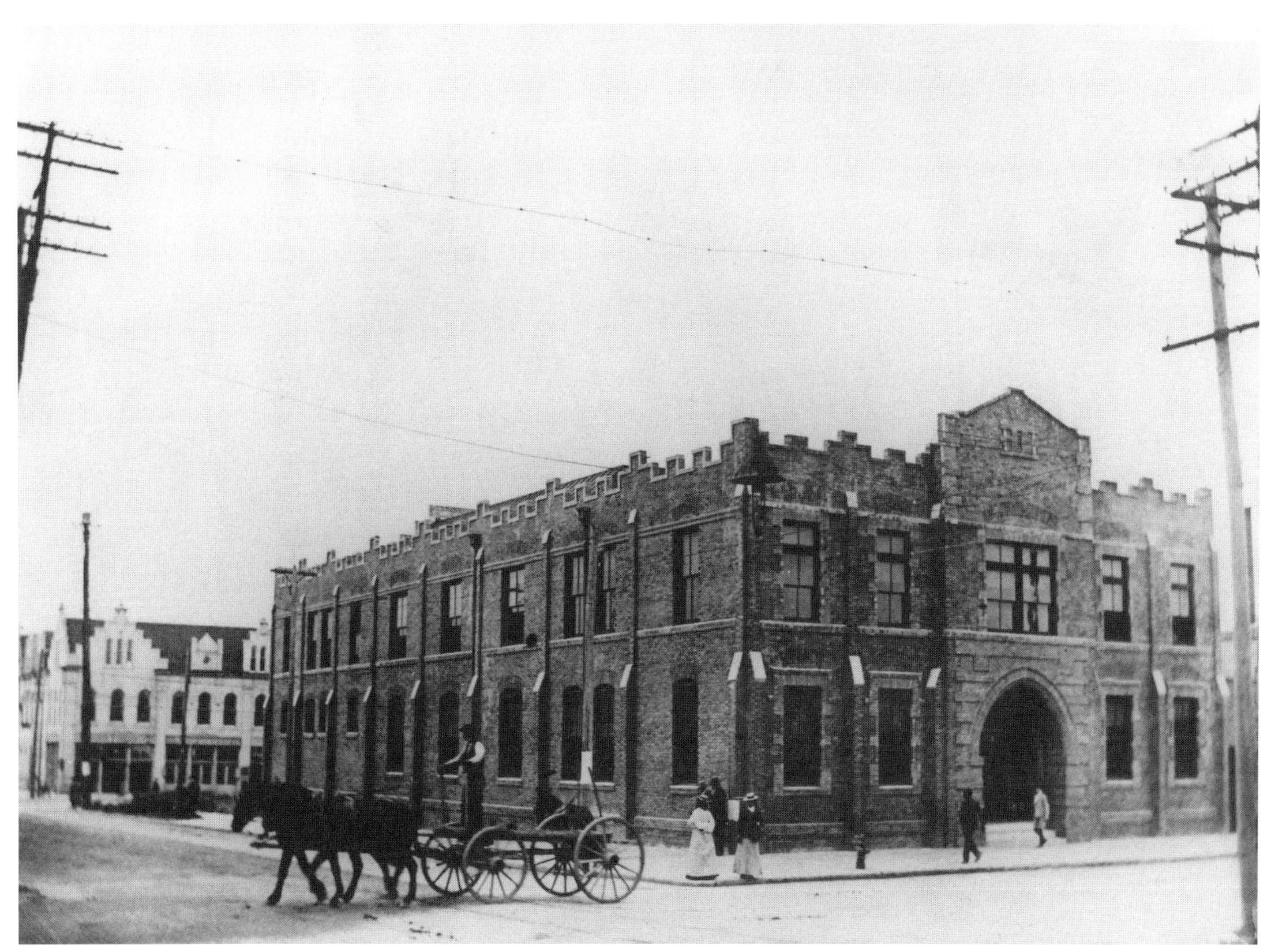

Jacksonville Police Station and Jail, built after the Great Fire, was in use until it was torn down in 1927 to make way for the Florida Theatre.

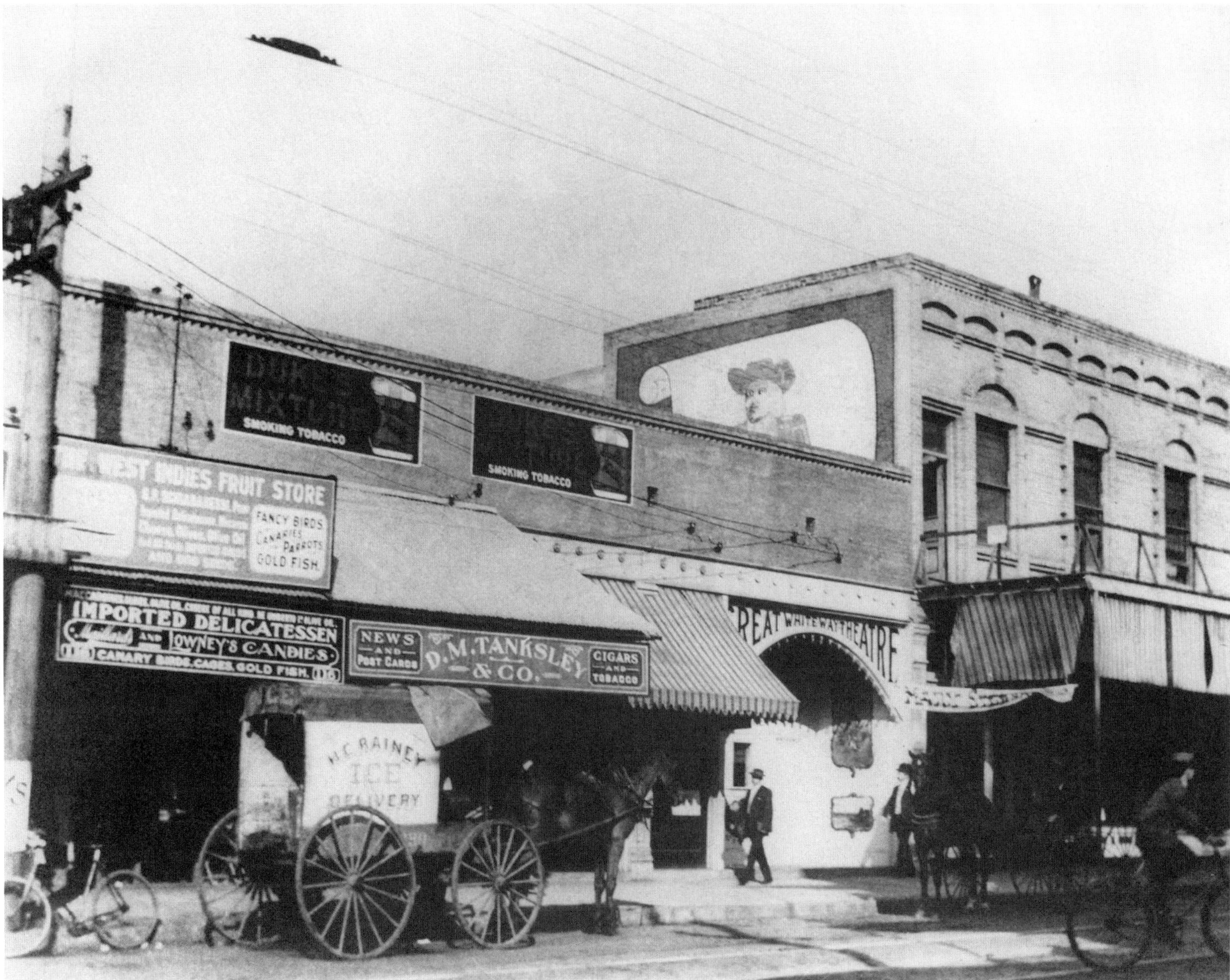

The Great White Way Theatre is tucked next to a tobacco shop and a delicatessen and fruit store that offered "fancy birds, canaries, parrots, and gold fish" along with apples and oranges. The horse-drawn wagon is delivering block ice.

house on Fishweir Creek, there must remain the bones of the original house that Leah Mary Cox built in 1919. But it is long grown over with additions and rearrangements of the space as new generations of the family have come along and shaped the house to shifting needs and improving fortune.

Lenah Scott Geiger, Leah Cox's niece, lives there now. Lenah and her sister, Alice Scott Jones, born in the first decades of the twentieth century, study a photograph of the young Leah taken in her house-building years or earlier—square-jawed, spectacles, a confident grin. Strength and good humor. A friendly, sociable face.

The nieces shake their heads. "That is not the Auntsie Leah we knew," Lenah Geiger observes. "I remember her as very old. And very stern."

"Children were to be seen and not heard," Alice Jones confirms. "You were supposed to do what you were told to do."

"She was the matriarch," Lenah Geiger acknowledged. Matriarch. Now, there's a title with an imperial ring.

Leah Cox didn't inherit the title simply by growing into it. If she ruled the Cox roost—and by all accounts she did—it was because she took charge of her family when there was no one else to take charge.

That young woman is far beyond recalling by her nieces. Looking for Leah Cox is not a simple stroll down memory lane. Her nieces must dig for a glimpse of her, an echo of her. Cox was eighty-six years old when she died in 1953. After almost fifty years, who is much remembered in any detail? A name, a few dates on documents can be searched out. Birth certificate, baptismal certificate, marriage certificate, death certificate.

We could find Leah Mary Cox's records of birth and baptism in Cirencester, England, where she was born. But we would not find a marriage certificate with her name on it anywhere. Her family came ready-made, surely a daunting tribe to a suitor, although, apparently, there was a suitor. There is a tale that she loved a soldier who died in the Spanish-American War. There is no name to go with the story of the soldier, but the story is consistent and as old as any memory of Leah Cox. And the possibility of a romance fits the times and fits her circumstances at the time.

The Spanish-American War was Jacksonville's war.

The city was a hotbed of intrigue and activity during the period leading to the war and during the war. For years, anti-Spanish, pro-Cuban independence activists operated from Jacksonville. Local political leaders were among the first in the United States to go on record condemning Spain for its boot on the neck of Cuba.

Headquarters of the Cuban revolutionary junta in Florida was in Jacksonville. Jose Marti, the liberator of Cuba, was often in the city. The gunrunning sea-going tugs,

Three Friends, *Dauntless*, *Bermuda*, and *Commodore*, sailed out of Jacksonville, delivering goods by the ton to fight a war.

Passion for the cause of Cuban independence was high throughout the United States, and there was a special intensity in Florida, with Cuba less than a hundred miles from the Keys, and innumerable commercial and family connections between the countries. Volunteers to throw the Spanish out were plentiful. All that was needed was an incident, and a declaration of war.

Remember the *Maine*.

The U.S. battleship *Maine* exploded in Havana harbor in February 1898, killing 260 American sailors. Spain was the prime suspect. Passion was whipped up with "evidence" that the ship was sunk by a Spanish torpedo. The U.S. press, particularly the newspapers of William Randolph Hearst and Joseph Pulitzer, reported with no shred of doubt that Spain did it, and pushed for war. "Remember the *Maine*—To Hell with Spain" was their fin de siècle mantra, a rallying cry for war.

Spain countered that there was no torpedo, and decades later that was proved to be so. However, dead sailors and the wreckage of the *Maine* rusting half-sunk in Havana harbor spoke louder in 1898 than the proceedings of a fact-finding commission, especially a Spanish commission.

War was declared in April. Jacksonville was a natural to be one of six assembly points for troops on the East Coast, and the citizenry invited, indeed urged, the army to set up camp in the city.

Camp Cuba Libre was established in East Springfield on the railroad tracks, bordered by Third, Eighth, and Ionia Streets. Maj. Gen. Fitzhugh Lee was in command; Camp Cuba Libra was headquarters to the Seventh Corps.

Military units from Wisconsin, Illinois, Virginia, North Carolina, and Iowa poured in by train and paraded through town on the way to Camp Cuba Libre. Saloon keepers, ladies of the evening, women of the Temperance Union, small boys, society matrons and their daughters, and tradespeople of all kinds cheered them on.

Perhaps Cox's suitor was among these men at arms.

It is possible that he was a member of one of the Jacksonville military companies—the Jacksonville Light Infantry and the Jacksonville Rifles—that left in mid-May for Tampa. But, if he were a Jacksonville man, it seems unlikely that, in a hundred years, his identity would not have become known. The fact that the name of the soldier and the details of his life and death and of his courtship of Cox are unknown would seem to favor the notion that he was an out-of-towner, just in the city for the war. Col. Jay L. Torrey's Second Wyoming Cavalry, also known as the Rocky Mountain Boys, were stationed in Jacksonville. They were rowdy westerners, but the city, caught in patriotic

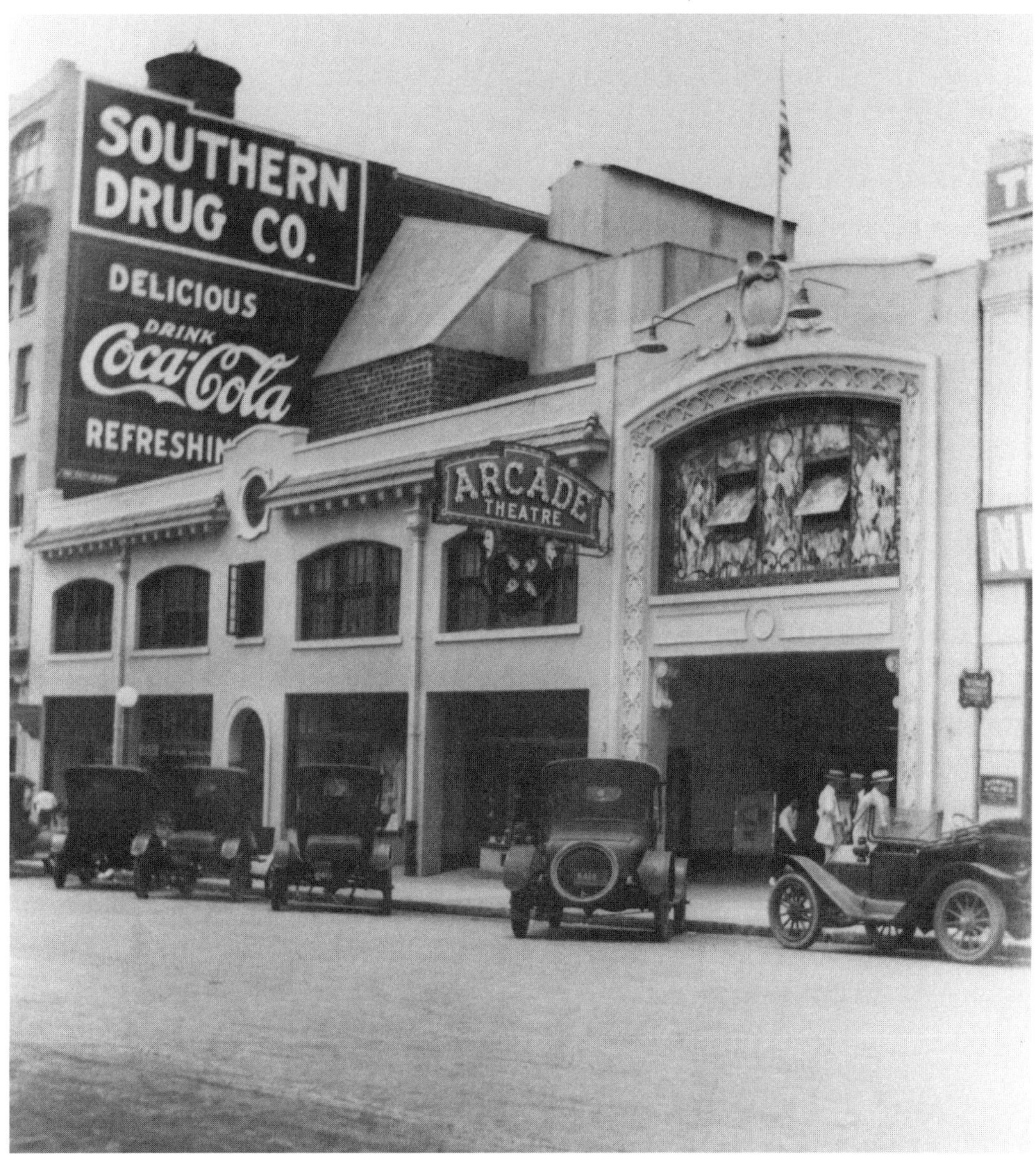

Ever fascinated by the city's entertainment venues, Cox photographed the Arcade Theatre along with the Southern Drug Company's ad for Coke; by this time, horses and buggies had given way to automobiles on Jacksonville streets.

excitement and war fever, took the troops and their commander to heart. A welcome banquet for Torrey at the Windsor Hotel was, one newspaper reported, "attended by everybody of any significance whatsoever." A glittering reception at the Seminole Club for officers of the Seventh Corps was described as the most elegant social event in the history of the city, and most likely of the state.

Perhaps Leah Cox was there. She must have attended some of the social events planned to entertain the soldiers. The social side of war would surely keep Jacksonville's three hundred dressmakers busy—and aware of what was going on, who was going to which parties and with whom, and what they wore. Events were constant. The movement of troops in and out of Jacksonville—almost thirty thousand before the "splendid little war" was over—was constant. Business zoomed out of sight; merchants sold supplies—lumber, feed grain and hay, wash buckets, tobacco, whiskey, vegetables, eggs, canned peaches—to the troops. Fortunes were made, and, as in any economic boom, there was trickle down. Musicians, caterers, newspaper correspondents, and dressmakers prospered.

Somewhere in the heady atmosphere, Cox met a man who became part of the story of her life, albeit it is in many ways a mystery story.

Here is what is agreed on: He was a soldier. She went, more than once, to visit him in Key West. He died in the war.

Mary Jane Hebard Cox was a young bride—the wife of Rowland Cox's son—and Auntsie Leah was an old woman when they met, on a Thanksgiving visit to the family almost sixty years ago. Mary Jane Cox was a nervous newcomer; Leah Cox was the stern matriarch of the family. They found a common thread when Mary Jane mentioned growing up near Valisparia, Nebraska, where Leah had grown up.

Later, when Mary Jane returned to Miami, she reported on her meeting with Leah Cox to a friend and, in one of those convergences of experience that seem too odd to be mere coincidence, her friend's mother overheard. Whoa! she said. She knew Leah Cox. In the old days, in Key West. Leah had stayed with her family—the Key West pioneer cigar-making DuBruiel family—when she had come to town to visit her friend. In addition, the DuBruiel family had, for a time, left Key West when the cigar factory closed and come to Jacksonville and rented space from Cox in a large house on Church Street where the Cox family lived and where Leah Cox sublet space to tenants.

The notion of Auntsie Leah, so stern, so rigid, as a young woman in love is not a perfect fit, but no one disbelieves it. No one, however, seems ever to have heard a word of the story from Cox herself.

"Auntsie Leah was hard to communicate with," says Mary Jane Cox, confirming the consensus. Memories of those who knew her, or who have heard tell of her, are sketchy and fading every year.

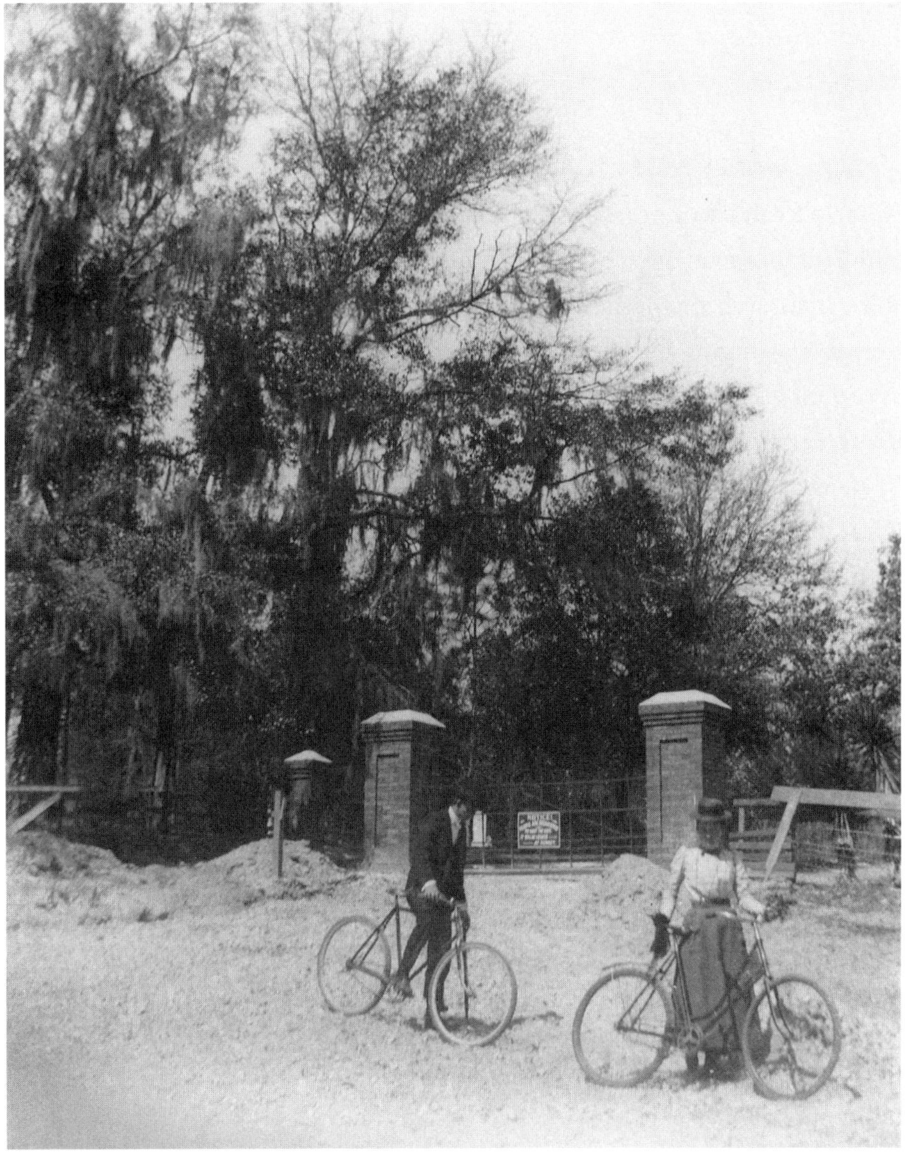

Bicyclists pause at the gates of Evergreen Cemetery during its expansion. When she could manage it, Cox had the bodies of her father and a brother moved from Tallahassee to Evergreen, where she was later buried.

Linus Scott, the brother of Lenah Geiger and Alice Jones, carries a lasting impression of Leah Cox's orderly mind, but few personal memories of her.

"She was very exacting. We kids had to pose for her, and our cousins from Miami had to pose. And she was very precise about arranging the photographs," he said.

Her hat-making told him she was imaginative and fanciful.

But her photographs tell a story of rigid discipline.

Linus Scott, like others who remember Cox, does not remember her as a warm person. His Aunt Lenah, with whom Leah Cox lived, was by far the more approachable of the women.

"The two of them were very unusual individuals. My thoughts are that Auntsie Lenah, the younger of the two, kind of felt obligated to take care of Auntsie Leah in her last years. Oh, Auntsie Leah was the boss, but I think perhaps Auntsie Lenah was taking care of Auntsie Leah."

Lenah Cox was younger, but she was by no means young, and it was Lenah who literally moved tons of sand, in a small wagon—some say a child's wagon, others an old ice cream wagon—from a pile at the street around to the banks of the Fishweir Creek behind the house to stabilize low spots. Tirelessly, it seemed. Leah was mostly indoors, sewing and cooking, possibly, by this time, troubled with heart disease from which she suffered for the last ten years of her life.

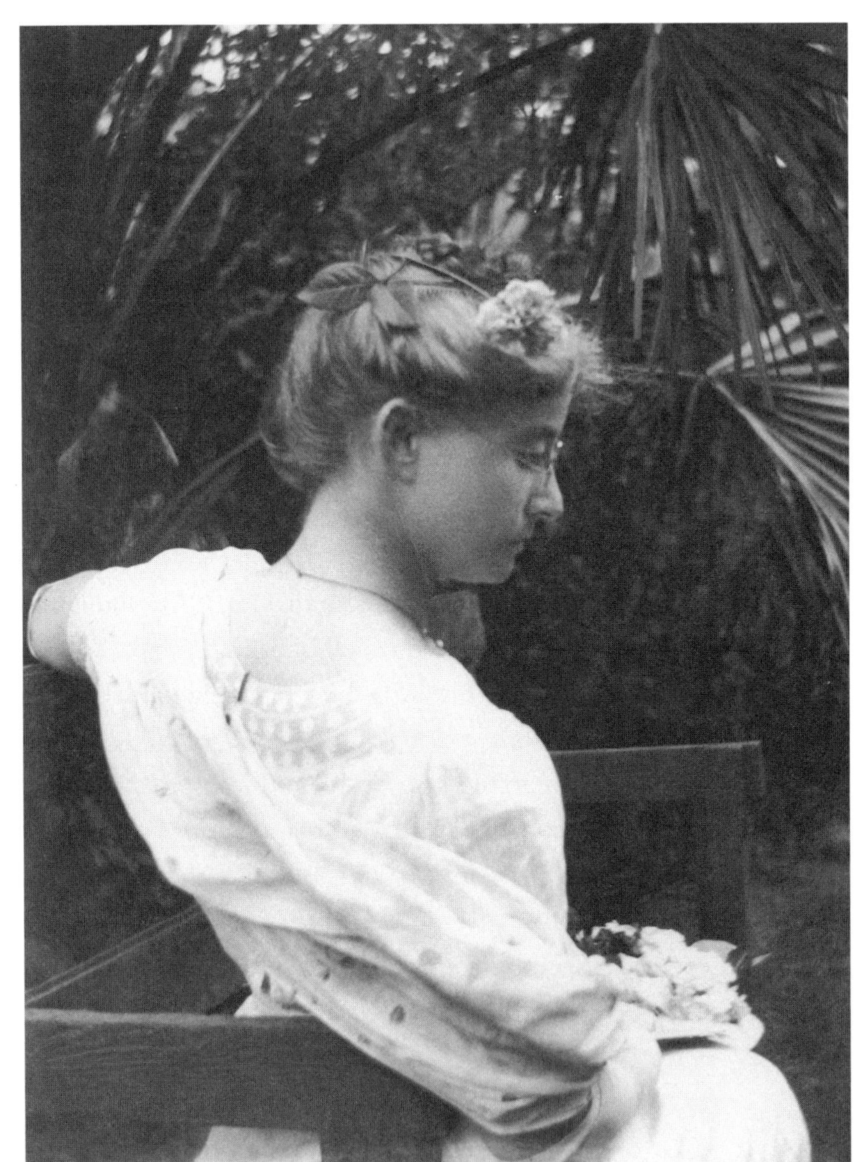

Leah Mary Cox as a young woman, and in 1923, at fifty-six.

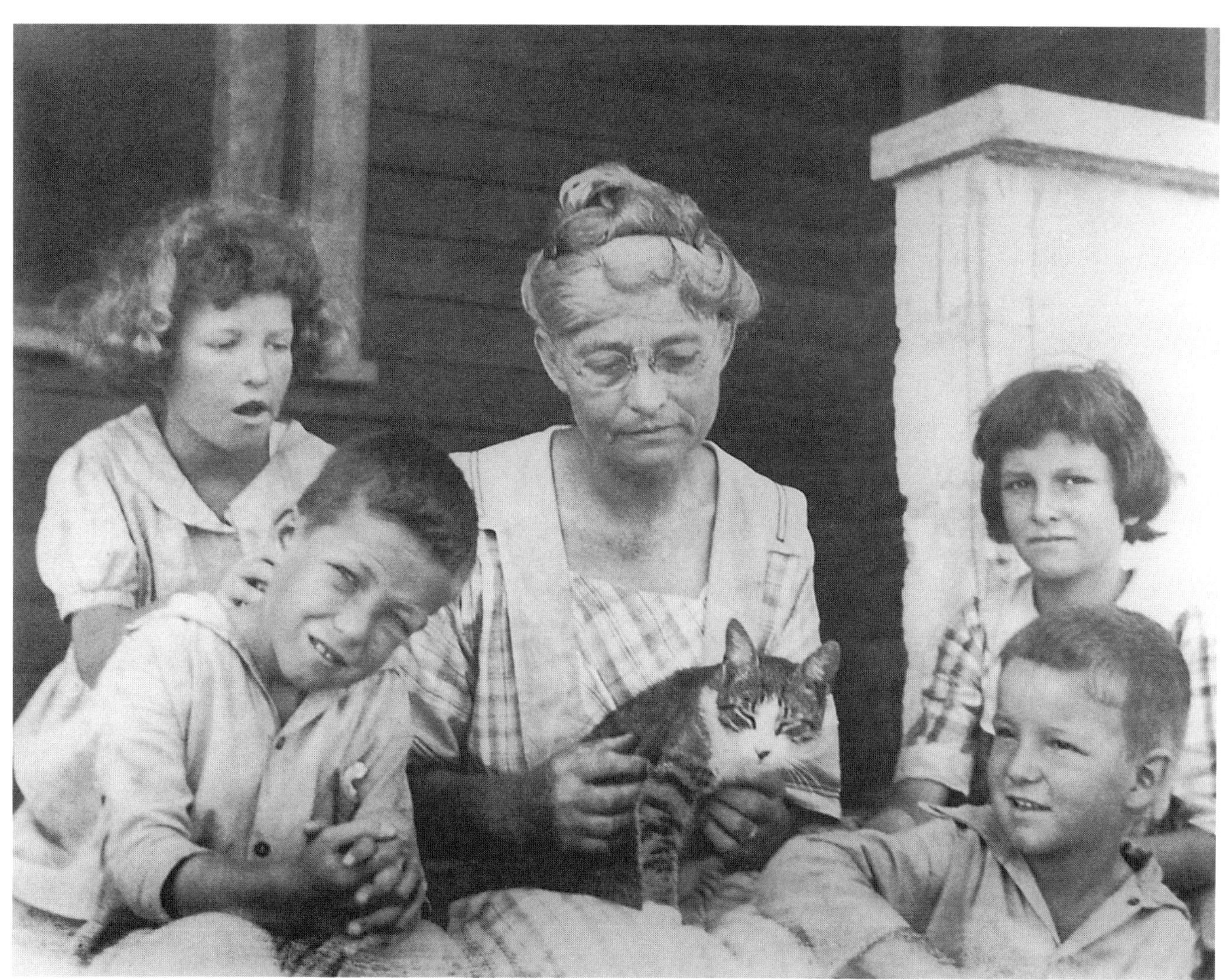

“She was like a grandmother, age-wise,” her nieces say.

She still lined the kids up for photographs, however. And she supervised their decorum and behavior. Lenah taught them to play card games. Leah taught them not to cuss—never “darn,” absolutely never “cripes.” Only an occasional “by jimminy” was okay. Leah Cox once chopped off Alice’s hair above the ears for neglecting to pin it back properly. By the time the nieces were aware of her as a photographer, she was taking pictures of family, and the kids whose parents she once took on as her life’s work were dodging her barbs. The days of climbing rooftops to get the picture were past for Leah Mary Cox.

“We were scared of her,” said Alice.

They should have known her when she stepped off the train from Tallahassee to begin a new life, carried a sick child on her back to shelter—as she assumed the care of her family—built a house with her own hands. And, always, got the picture.

BIBLIOGRAPHY

Barbour, George M. *Florida for Tourists, Invalids, and Settlers: Containing Practical Information Regarding Climate, Soil and Productions; Cities, Towns, and People; The Culture of the Orange etc.* A facsimile reproduction of the 1882 edition. Gainesville: University of Florida Press, 1964.

Crooks, James B. *Jacksonville After the Fire, 1901–1919.* Jacksonville: University of North Florida Press, 1991.

Foley, Bill, and M. Jack Luedke, eds. *Jacksonville: Images Through the 20th Century.* Jacksonville: Florida Times-Union, 1999.

Foley, Bill, and Wayne W. Wood. *The Great Fire of 1901.* Jacksonville: Jacksonville Historical Society, 2001.

Gannon, Michael. *Florida: A Short History.* Gainesville: University Press of Florida, 1993.

———, ed. *The New History of Florida.* Gainesville: University Press of Florida, 1996.

Hallam, George. *Riverside Remembered.* Jacksonville: Riverside Avondale Preservation, 1976.

Humphreys, Margaret. *Yellow Fever and the South.* Baltimore: Johns Hopkins University Press, 1992.

Stowe, Harriet Beecher. *Palmetto Leaves.* Boston: James R. Osgood, 1873.

Ward, James Robertson, with Dena Elizabeth Snodgrass. *Old Hickory's Town: An Illustrated History of Jacksonville.* Jacksonville: Old Hickory's Town, 1985.

Webb, Wanton S., ed. and comp. *Webb's Historical Industrial and Biographical Florida, Part I.* New York: W. S. Webb, 1885.

———. *Webb's Jacksonville and Consolidated Directory of Representative Cities in East and South Florida 1887.* Jacksonville: W. S. Webb, 1887.

WPA Writer's Program. *Jacksonville and Duval County History from Miscellaneous Sources.* Vol. 5. Manuscript, P. K. Yonge Library of Florida History, University of Florida, Gainesville. 1939.

Ann Hyman is a former general assignment and feature writer and columnist for the *Florida Times-Union* and editor of the *Times-Union* Sunday book review page. She has also written a novel, *The Lansing Legacy*, and a memoir, *Chaos Clear as Glass.*